Vivien Leigh

Vivien Leigh

John Russell Taylor

Photographs from the
KOBAL COLLECTION

ST MARTIN'S PRESS
New York

For William
This fruit of a long-shared devotion

Design by Craig Dodd

ISBN 0–312–85070–0
Library of Congress Catalog Number: 84–50679

Contents

Introduction

I met Vivien Leigh only once. It was in the line of duty, as I was
called upon to interview her. I did not take to her terribly, nor
did she, obviously, to me. Our exchange was short and, undeniably, sharp – which took me rather by surprise, because I
am anything but what is called an attacking interviewer. And yet
in retrospect it ties up in my mind with her particular and very
special qualities as an actress and as a star. There are, it seems,
certain wrestlers who decide early in their career to cast themselves as the anti-body, the performers who never play for
sympathy, but remain proudly aloof from all questions of whether
the audience likes them, is with them, or not. Vivien Leigh on
stage and screen often had something of that same proud defiance.

It was not, certainly, that she took the relatively easy way of
being the star you love to hate; she did not choose to play villains
any more than she chose to play sympathy-traps. Her speciality
was that sort of character which requires an audience's appraisal
rather than its involvement. Most actors demand, directly or
indirectly, that the audience should be drawn in: if they cannot

love, at least they can hate. Vivien Leigh, almost alone of the major stars, seemed able to live in a world of her own, unconcerned with what people really felt about her or the characters she portrayed.

This, obviously, was why she was the best imaginable Scarlett O'Hara. Any of the other contestants for the part would surely have weighted the character too much one way or the other, guiding the audience's sympathies. Vivien Leigh simply *was*, as Scarlett was, superbly unconcerned about how we might judge her. If one may follow this line further, it is to see in all Vivien Leigh's great roles – Lady Hamilton, Anna Karenina, Blanche Dubois, Mrs Treadwell in *Ship of Fools* – something of the same private quality, the same detachment.

One of the obituaries took the line that Vivien Leigh was not perhaps much of an actress, but at least she was a great star. That seems to me putting the cart before the horse. She was a great star, of course (didn't she win two Oscars?), but she managed to be one in spite of lacking nearly all the qualities which make for

easy audience acceptance. She was beautiful, certainly, and magnetic. But she never lost a certain coldness; she was small, sharp, crystal-clear; she was not easy to love, not over-eager to charm, not at all comfortable. She forced respect because she did not beg for anything. She knew her limitations and rarely (only as Lady Macbeth and as Shakespeare's Cleopatra, perhaps) over-stepped them. And what she did she did immaculately well, with perfect command of her craft. It is difficult to think of a star who has been more completely an actress, less readily a mere personality. Like her? Not necessarily. But miss her? We shall all do that.

*　*　*　*

Called upon to produce some kind of obituary, I wrote that at the time of Vivien Leigh's death, and would not want to change a word of it now, seventeen years later, except to express, more clearly than I originally had space to, my own private reservations on the then general opinion that her Lady Macbeth was a miscalculation. (I never saw her as Shakespeare's Cleopatra.) What the passage of time has made clearer, though, is her irreplaceability. There never was, and never has been since, anyone remotely like her on the British stage or the English-speaking screen. Since her death we have learnt a lot about her private life and her personal problems which was not common knowledge at the time. Almost too much, for though it makes a story of undeniable human interest, like the very different revelations about the family life of Joan Crawford it makes little or no difference to our evaluation of her professional career, even if it can only increase our respect for the almost supernatural discipline and control with which she left physical and mental suffering behind the moment she walked on to a stage. Even less now than before does she need – let alone ask for – anything she would despise so much as our pity. Her story is still a triumph: the more so now that we fully realise against what odds that triumph was achieved.

The Big Yes

Almost from the outset, Vivien Leigh's greatest disadvantage as well as her greatest advantage was her beauty. She answers perfectly Tolstoy's description of Anna Karenina as a woman so beautiful that men and women would stop and look at her in the street, as she passed. After her death Roger Furse, a friend and sometimes professional associate, summed up what seems to have been quite a widely-held belief when he wrote 'I don't suppose that up to the sad break-up with L. [Laurence Olivier] she had ever had a serious "No" said to her since she was born.' On a certain level this is no doubt true: It is hard to say a personal No, and often very difficult to say a professional No, to a person of transcendent beauty. And let us not quibble about words. Though there were those who said that she was the quintessence of prettiness or piquancy rather than a true classical beauty, for her combination of looks and charisma only 'beauty' will really do. But along with all the small immediate assents, there was nearly always the one big important reservation lurking behind. Because she was beautiful, could she have talent as well? She undoubtedly decorated a stage, but could she act? She had the sort of striking, individual personality that lights up a screen, but could she play anyone but herself? Throughout her professional life she was plagued with the sort of luke-warm judgment that starts 'Oh, she looks wonderful, I grant you, but ...' And that, it seems to me, was the persistent rumbling No which tended to invalidate for her all the clearly articulated Yeses.

Even if this were so, there must obviously have been times in her career when it did not seem so important. Like the moment when she heard the biggest and most decisive Yes of all – the decision that she, out of all possible and impossible actresses in the world, should play the most sought-after role in the most talked-about movie of the decade, *Gone With the Wind*. That was in the New Year of 1939 and she was just twenty-six. She had, curiously enough, just had a firm and unexpected No in London. The great French stage director Michel Saint-Denis had been planning, earlier in 1938, a major revival of Chekhov's *Three Sisters* as part of John Gielgud's season at the Queen's Theatre. Peggy Ashcroft was going to play Irina, Gwen Ffrangcon-Davies would play Olga, and Vivien Leigh thought she ought to play Masha. So did almost everyone else, as it happened, but Saint-Denis would not hear of it. Whatever anybody else might say, he would not, could not concede that this dazzling young beauty had any talent, even though half the young men in London were publicly in love with her, and one important particular star, Laurence Olivier, was keeping his (reciprocated) passion as much of a secret as, in the circumstances, it could possibly be. But to let her loose on Chekhov? For Saint-Denis it was sacrilege, and he said so in no uncertain terms. The role went, instead, to a notable though now forgotten American stage actress, Carol Goodner, and Vivien, nursing her wounded ego, went into a short-lived trifle called *Serena Blandish*, adapted by S. N. Behrman from an elegantly artificial novel by Enid Bagnold.

Not, mind you, that 1938 had been a wholly disastrous year for her, or anything like. She had appeared in two British films, *A Yank at Oxford* and *St Martin's Lane*, both of them, quite exceptionally for British films, successful in America as well as Britain. She was not yet a star, not quite, but she was getting there. And off in the distance somewhere was this big chance, the possibility of playing Scarlett O'Hara. Or perhaps one should rather say, the impossibility of it. Attempts to cast the role had been going on with gradually increasing intensity since 1936, when David O. Selznick had been thinking of 'someone like' Miriam Hopkins or Tallulah Bankhead even before he had definitely bought the novel for filming. For two full years the search had gone on, milked for maximum publicity by Selznick's genius of PR Russell Birdwell. Virtually everyone in Hollywood, likely and unlikely, had been tested in key scenes, including such established stars as

The title role in Serena Blandish *at the Gate Theatre*

Jean Arthur and Margaret Sullavan, as well as nobodies who would one day be somebodies, like Lana Turner and Susan Hayward. (Bette Davis, whom many readers of the book wanted, was contractually out of the question, and another front-runner, Katharine Hepburn, steadfastly refused to test.) With all this good ole American beauty and talent available, why should the role go to a relatively unknown English girl, however gorgeous? But, Vivien thought, she could dream, couldn't she? When the brief run of *Serena Blandish* came to an end, she was restless. Laurence Olivier was in Hollywood playing Heathcliff in *Wuthering Heights* – he, of course, had thought she would be ideal as Cathy, but the film's producers had naturally wanted to know why they should cast a nobody when they had Merle Oberon. On impulse, more or less, Vivien decided to hurry over to visit Olivier, and coincidentally see what could be done about getting the role of Scarlett. After all, Selznick must be now be nearly desperate as shooting had already started on secondary scenes, and it was the moment when a complete outsider probably had the best chance. She took ship to New York, and from there a plane to Clover Field Airport, Los Angeles. Olivier met her, crouching for discretion's sake in the back of an anonymous car just outside the airport gates.

As far as *Gone With the Wind* was concerned, her arrival was not totally unprepared. Olivier had dropped a few heavy hints about her to his American agent, who happened to be Myron Selznick, the brother of David O. Myron staged things with his customary care. The story has been told a thousand times – despite which it seems to be in outline absolutely true. According to Hitchcock, Selznick faked the later much-publicised search for an actress to play the nameless heroine of *Rebecca*, having already at the outset decided on Joan Fontaine. But with Scarlett he played it straight because he had little alternative. All his tests had failed to produce the one obvious, unarguable choice. And there they were already shooting the burning of Atlanta, everything with three different stand-ins for Scarlett, to cover all eventualities of final casting. All this was witnessed by three visitors to the set, Myron Selznick, Laurence Olivier and Vivien Leigh – but so discreetly that Selznick brusquely noted at the time when writing to his wife in New York, 'Myron rolled in just exactly too late, arriving about a minute and a half after the last building had fallen and burned and after the shots were comleted.' But there was method in his madness. While the light from the last flames flickered becomingly over Vivien's perfect features and imparted just the right auburn tinge to her dark hair, he marched her over to his brother and announced dramatically 'David, meet Scarlett O'Hara!' Olivier records that he thought (or prayed) 'David won't be able to resist that' – and sure enough he wasn't. A couple of days later Selznick confided to his wife 'Shhhhh, she's the Scarlett dark horse, and looks damned good.' When the final, decisive tests were made that same week George

Photographed by Laszlo Willinger in costume for Gone With the Wind. *MGM*

Cukor directed her along with the other 'finalists', Paulette Goddard, Jean Arthur and Joan Bennett. Selznick had promised to make every possible allowance for her still deficient Southern accent, but there was no inherent reason to suppose that any of the others, just because they happened to be American, would automatically do it to the manner born. And in the event there was really no contest: Cukor was excited from the outset by the 'indescribable wildness about her', which was so true to the essential Scarlett. Seeing the identical test scenes of the four actresses again today one is not for a moment surprised that she got the role. On 13 January the announcement drafted on 4 January was made public, and principal photography on the film began 25 January.

That, at any rate is the official story, and there is no denying that it does sound more like romantic fiction than hard business-like fact. But then it has always been part of Hollywood's charm and strength that it could, when necessary, believe its own carefully nurtured myths, and even act on them. Obviously some

Vivien signs the contract, watched by David O. Selznick, Leslie Howard and Olivia de Havilland

of the coincidences were carefully contrived. A few days after her arrival Vivien was writing with elaborate casualness to her then husband Leigh Holman 'You will never guess what has happened – and no one is more surprised than me – you know how I only came out here for a week – well, just two days before I was supposed to leave, the people who are making *Gone With the Wind* saw me and said would I make a test – so what could I do? ...' (And the disingenuous tone, it must be noted, did not come from a need to be secret about her relations with Olivier, since Holman was completely *au courant* and reconciling himself to divorce.) But undoubtedly a determination to play Scarlett was a very important reason for her being in Hollywood from the outset – if still secondary to her need to see Olivier.

Once Myron Selznick had been convinced of her theoretical suitability for the role, the whole meeting with David was meticulously stage-managed, from the precise timing of their arrival on the lot after dinner at Chasin's to the details of her wardrobe – a large hat to frame her face in an appropriately period manner, a

Walter Plunkett fits Vivien Leigh in one of his designs (the notorious red dress) for Gone With the Wind

dress unusually cinched in at the waist to show off her ability to wear Scarlett's clothes, and even the unusual shade of green eyeshadow she wore that evening. David Niven, who was appearing in *Wuthering Heights* with Olivier, recalled meeting her that fateful week, when she was waiting to hear about the role, and characterised her then as 'a Dresden beauty and *quite* sure she would get it!' It was certainly more than possible she would get it, but it was no forgone conclusion, whatever she thought. George Cukor, though he conveniently 'forgot' in the flood of enthusiasm with which she was launched, had been in Britain a few months before, seen *A Yank at Oxford* and when asked by an interviewer what he thought of Britain's new beauty replied unenthusiastically that 'she seems to be a little static, not quite sufficiently fiery for the role.' And Selznick, still enthusing the week after he had met Vivien about the possibilities Jean Arthur was showing during her final tests (incomprehensibly if one looks at the insufferably coy results on film), took more selling on the idea, more careful consultation with other interests involved, before he finally decided.

Through it all Vivien seemed quite imperturbable, playing the innocent with her husband, the confident careerist with David Niven, the troubled idealist with Tyrone Guthrie (she had to get out of playing Titania in his new London production of *A Midsummer Night's Dream*, since however the decision went she could not get back in time for rehearsals) and the single-minded lover with Olivier – though to do her justice, there clearly was no need to 'play' that particular role. No one knew what she was really thinking and feeling, not even, probably, herself, and if Cukor hoped or expected the mask would drop when he teased for a moment or two before telling her at his 1938 Christmas Party 'Well, I guess we're stuck with you!' he was disappointed. Of course she was delighted, but then she knew so perfectly how to produce the proper, charming reaction to a kindly uncle who has just given you a lovely gift. Of course, this was *just* what she had always wanted ...

Though it was charming to say thank you prettily at the right time, Vivien was never, for a moment, a person whose reactions could be taken for granted. If she found it easy to behave like Scarlett on screen, it was quite possibly because she found it easy to behave that way off. It is impossible not to hear the accents of Scarlett O'Hara in her letters to Leigh Holman, with their headlong punctuation and seemingly random but strangely artful succession of ideas, impulses and indications. It was normal at the time, and indeed up to Vivien's death in 1967, if not much beyond, to regard all this as not only enchanting, but necessarily feminine. Nowadays, our consciousness suitably raised by feminism, it is difficult to know what this nexus of ideas should be called. But in a period sense there is no doubt that Vivien Leigh was the acme of feminity, delightful, maddening and of course, by definition, incomprehensible to any mere man. When she complained, in

Rhett and Scarlett. Clarence Sinclair Bull/MGM

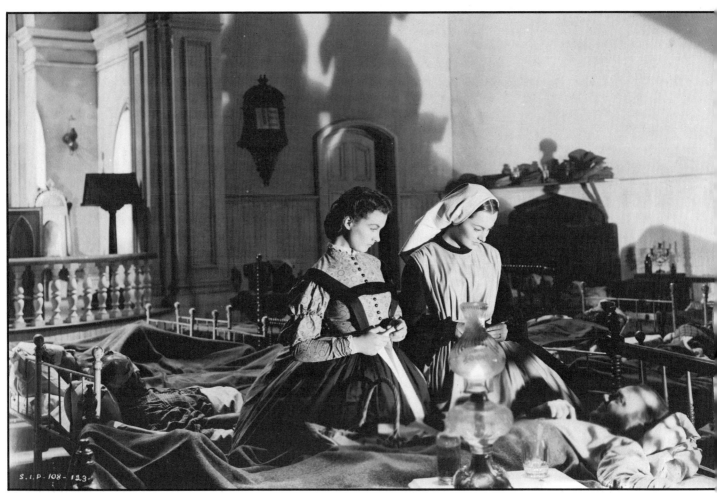

Opposite: *on duty and off during*
Gone With the Wind, *with Olivia de*
Havilland (above) *and Clark Gable*
and Victor Fleming (below).
Below: *Vivien's perilous tangle with*
the stampeding horses.
Fred Parrish/MGM

letters home, that 'As you so well realise, I loathe Hollywood ...' it is pointless to enquire whether or not she really meant it. Naturally, she did and she didn't. She had a driving ambition, which was for the moment being well satisfied.

On the other hand, her famous temperament was already on occasion giving cause for alarm. She accepted quite well the first major upset once production proper was under way on *Gone With the Wind* – the unceremonious firing of George Cukor as director after only ten days. She might complain to Leigh that 'He was my last hope of ever enjoying the picture,' but the prognostication was as usual exaggerated – a stamp of the little foot (or the not-so-little foot, as she was always oddly self-conscious about the disproportionate size of her hands and feet) and she was off and going again. She persuaded Cukor to read important scenes with her in secret (and so, she discovered, did the film's Melanie, Olivia de Havilland), and then set herself the task of charming the man's-man Victor Fleming who replaced him. She also found it easy to get on with Clark Gable, who played Rhett Butler. (He let her teach him backgammon – or did he teach her? Nobody seems quite sure, though there was no doubt that whenever they played it, she won.) Olivia de Havilland became a personal friend, but her relations with Leslie Howard, who played her hopeless love Ashley Wilkes, were more problematical, and in the film it sometimes shows.

But the main source of trouble, when it came, seems to have been Laurence Olivier's absence in New York. Once he had finished *Wuthering Heights* he decided it would not be wise from a career point of view to stick around in Hollywood, dancing attendance. Nor would it be exactly discreet, since though by this time their attachment was more or less an open secret (the affair had, after all, been going on since 1935, and both were now involved in arranging divorces) in Hollywood a respectable face still had to be put on things. So, he seized the opportunity to star on Broadway with Katherine Cornell in *No Time for Comedy*, a new play, curiously enough, by the same S. N. Behrman who had written Vivien's last London play. This one, however, was a major success, and looked like keeping Olivier tied up on the other side of the continent for a considerable time. Before that could even become evident, however, trouble struck: a combination of exhaustion and hysteria took Vivien out of the shooting for an indeterminate period, with a fortune threatened the longer they had to shoot around her. There was nothing for it but that he should heed Selznick's desperate call, skip the dress rehearsal in Indianapolis (where the play was about to have its out-of-town opening), fly to Los Angeles, spend a day there soothing and comforting and then fly back for the first night. The visit – or the drama of it all – apparently did the trick. Olivier went back to triumph, and Vivien went back to the gruelling schedule which sometimes had her shooting round the clock, seven days a week, skipping backwards and forwards in fictional time as the piece-

meal nature of the shooting required. Meanwhile writers came and went, scripts were dissolved and reconstituted, cameramen hired and fired, and even the he-man Fleming collapsed and had to be replaced, then supplemented by other directors.

All things considered, it is remarkable that she managed to miss only five days' shooting during twenty-two weeks of principal photography. No wonder she wrote to Leigh 'I will never get used to this – how I *hate* film acting!' To enhance the drama some

of the big action scenes required that the star should be unmistakably recognisable in the midst, and Vivien herself had to do a number of hazardous things which would normally have been left to a stand-in or a stunt-girl. She seems to have taken risks with stampeding horses and the general chaos of beleaguered Atlanta that made bystanders fear for her life, and to have done them without turning a hair. Though she was playing the star role, and *Gone With the Wind* is essentially Scarlett's story, however important others may be in it, she was not yet a star: the release of the film would be the real test of that. She was not even, yet, being paid a star's salary - only $20,000, since Selznick cannily maintained he would be a laughing-stock if he paid an unknown any more for taking the chance of a lifetime.

Did she already behave like a star, though? At least she behaved always like herself, which meant that from time to time she could display star temperament as well as anyone. Occasionally her temper or her tongue would run away with her. Once, for instance, when Victor Fleming was directing, they came to the scene between Scarlett and Ashley after the defeat of the South which had been one of the major test scenes. For some reason it would not come right, and by the middle of the afternoon she got so irritated that she turned on Fleming and not only announced that they should all go and see the test directed by Cukor to observe how it should be done, but actually forced Fleming to do this. More, perhaps, the way a pampered, established star would behave than a vulnerable beginner eager to please. However, her ways of pleasing were always on her own terms. She could relate well enough to Fleming and Gable, both rather self-consciously (and perhaps not too securely) very masculine, because she clearly did not represent any sexual challenge to them (all her sexual energies were wrapped up with Olivier at this time, insofar as they did not go into her performance) and she could, it was well-known, swear them both under the table if the mood took her. If there were any gaps and moments of collapse, they were evidently genuine rather than strategic and she was professional enough to recover rapidly from them, this side of total exhaustion (in fact, ironically, it was the apparently tough Fleming who was carried off first). And even her troubles could be turned to use: when she arrived at the studio all blotchy and puffy from crying at the painful parting from Olivier, off to his play in New York, Selznick and Fleming promptly rescheduled the scene in which she has to cry at the death of her first husband in the war, and let her weep to her heart's content.

Understandably, neither she nor Olivier could wait for their reunion. Olivier had to be told as soon as possible when, approximately, she would finish filming, so that he could give notice of when he would leave the company of *No Time for Comedy*. In due course it became clear that the shooting would be done with Scarlett (who of course is in nearly every scene of the film) around the end of June. Olivier gave notice for 3 July. In the event, Scarlett's last scene was completed on 27 July, in the morning. That same afternoon she shot another test for a role in a Selznick film, this time for the heroine in his forthcoming version of Daphne du Maurier's romantic bestseller *Rebecca*, which was already set to star (as of mid-June) none other than Laurence Olivier as the moody, mysterious hero. Vivien's reasons for wanting to play the role of the waiflike second Mrs de Winter were therefore on a personal level pretty obvious. But it was also a plum role – if at first glance, a totally unsuitable one for her. However, as Selznick confided to his business partner John Hay Whitney 'It is my personal feeling that she could never be right for the girl, but God knows it would solve a lot of problems if she was right, and I have too much respect for her ability as an actress, too much consideration for my own peace of mind during the months of August and September when a certain young man is in these parts, and too much appreciation of how good it would be for her future with us if she were to play *Rebecca*, to close the door on the possibility of her being right for it.'

Could she possibly succeed being cast against type like this? She demanded the chance to try in fairer conditions, and indeed, after she had arrived in New York and worked with Olivier for a few days on a test scene, another test was shot. The result, unfortunately for her, was no more convincing. Back in Hollywood, Selznick sought the advice of George Cukor on the casting, showing him all the tests without prejudice and expecting a disinterested judgment even though he recognised that Cukor was 'a great enthusiast of Vivien's and a great personal friend of hers.' Cukor was in fact so disinterested that he watched all the tests in silence 'except for some loud guffaws at Vivien's attempts to play it', and then plumped for Joan Fontaine. As Selznick finally remarked, Vivien didn't 'seem at all right as to sincerity or age or innocence or any of the other factors which are essential to the story coming off at all.' Talent she had aplenty, but not enough to enter into the soul of Daphne du Maurier's timid innocent, whom she must always in her heart of hearts have regarded as a hopeless ninny.

One thing that had happened during Vivien's enforced separation from Olivier was that he had become a movie star, the genuine Hollywood model. With the release of *Wuthering Heights* he suddenly found himself a celebrity, of a very different kind from the dignified, limited celebrity of the Broadway theatre. When, in England a year earlier, he had asked his old friend Ralph Richardson whether he should take the role of Heathcliff or not, Richardson had thought for a moment, then uttered oracularly 'Yes. Bit of fame. Good.' Now his prediction had come true, it was good, but it also brought problems. Everyone in the world seemed to be avidly interested in Olivier's private life, as they had been increasingly during the last six months in Vivien's. It was doubtful how much longer they could remain even formally discreet enough to satisfy the sacrosanct double standards of

American show business, where an actress might be enjoyed playing the Whore of Babylon provided only that her private life was believed to be pure as the driven snow.

As soon as Olivier was free of *No Time for Comedy* (Vivien was able to sneak into his very last performance) and Vivien's final test for *Rebecca* was out of the way, they sailed, by chance as it were, on the same boat, the *Ile de France*, back to England for a month's holiday. They had some hope that both their divorces might be hurried through in this time, but things were not so easily arranged, and an indefinable air of impending doom hung over the country that August of 1939. They were already digging trenches in the parks and talking of air-raid precautions, just in case . . . The break was a blessed relief, but otherwise it was hardly in a comfortable frame of mind that they headed back to Hollywood and further secrecy, he to start *Rebecca*, she to finish a few retakes on *Gone With the Wind* before its opening, which was scheduled for December.

They arrived back in Hollywood on 23 August, the day the German-Soviet pact was signed and war in Europe became inevitable. Vivien's first scene in the reshooting was the one, early in the picture, where the sixteen-year-old Scarlett sits on the porch of Tara in a white dress and reflects petulantly that 'Everyone is talking of war, war, war.' When Selznick saw the rushes he immediately decided she looked too old and ill, and ordered her off for a holiday with Olivier to recuperate. Thus it was that they were cruising near Catalina in a yacht chartered by Douglas Fairbanks Jr, in the company of Vivien's mother and sundry other Britons such as David Niven, Robert Coote and Nigel Bruce, on 3 September, when they heard on the ship's radio that Britain and France were now at war with Germany. Olivier's uncharacteristic response was to get blind drunk and row himself round the Yacht Club harbour loudly prophesying doom: unfortunately his decided physical resemblance to Ronald Colman at that time landed Colman, who was moored nearby, with the blame for this very un-English disturbance. Vivien at once concluded they should all go home to England, but of course their respective professional commitments prevented them, and all they could do was to make sure that her mother, who had come out with them for the trip, should get back as quickly as possible. Despite all this, the little holiday did Vivien good, and she returned to the studio as radiantly young, healthy and beautiful as though she was in fact sixteen.

On 11 December Selznick cabled Kay Brown, his New York representative, 'Have just finished *Gone With the Wind*. God bless us one and all.' An urgent prayer, no doubt, since the première was due to take place on the 15th in Atlanta (where else?) with all the ballyhoo the combined forces of the Selznick organisation and MGM could possibly drum up. The day was declared an official state holiday by the governor of Georgia. Virtually the whole population of Atlanta was decked out in

Gone With the Wind première in *Atlanta: Olivia de Havilland with Jock Whitney, Vivien Leigh with Laurence Olivier*

After the Oscars: Vivien Leigh with Douglas Fairbanks Jr, Olivia de Havilland with Jock Whitney. The photographer, Laurence Olivier, is the recipient of the starry-eyed look

period costume for three days of parades and festivities, competition for tickets was so intense that they were changing hands for as much as $200 apiece instead of their face value of $10, and in advance Selznick fired off a record number of record-length cables to his minions covering everything down to the smallest details of the sort of paper to be used for the souvenir programme and the provision of non-noisy junk-food in the theatre.

And of course the stars were to be present. Leslie Howard was back in England already, but all the other principals were required to attend. Clark Gable's secret romance with Carole Lombard had now been rendered acceptable by their marriage, and they arrived in state in a plane specially chartered by MGM. On the other hand the Leigh/Olivier romance was still awaiting the same sort of prude-proof regularisation, and it looked as though Vivien would dig her heels in until Selznick came up with the idea that Olivier could legitimately come along for the ride to help publicise the now completed *Rebecca* as the next major Selznick release. So there they all were, with marching bands, fireworks, a glittering Atlanta ball and the works. It was just typical of Vivien, and one suspects not quite accidental, that as they stepped from the plane to the inevitable strains of 'Dixie' she was heard to observe sweetly 'Oh, they're playing the song from the picture!'

After all that, it was just to be hoped that the picture would be a success. But nobody, in his wildest dreams, could have foreseen quite how big a success it would be. Vivien did not exactly, like the archetypal show business hopeful in the archetypal putting-on-a-show movie, step on to that stage a nobody, and come off it a STAR, but such was the transformation wrought in her life and career by this one role that the public could be forgiven for seeing it that way. All at once, she was the most celebrated young woman in the world, or at least that part of it not already girding itself for war. And even in England the news of this triumph by a native daughter spread immediately, and made *Gone With the Wind* the most eagerly anticipated film since D.W. Griffith's *Intolerance*. The *New York Times* summed it all up when it said 'Vivien Leigh's Scarlett is so beautiful she hardly needs to be talented, and so talented she need not have been so beautiful.' The assessment was generous as well as just: Vivien had good cause to be satisfied. She was, and would always be, Scarlett O'Hara, and the balance of her looks and her skills had been accurately appraised. It was the big 'Yes' of her professional life, and it had come to her at the age of twenty-six. A wonderful way to begin. But there was a problem. Where did you go from there?

Morning Glory

For that matter, how did you get to this position in the first place? 'So I can't quite be called "Overnight Sensation", for it started many years ago . . .' throbbed Judy Garland in *A Star is Born*, and if Vivien Leigh cannot exactly be described as born in a trunk, she had certainly been, after a fashion, in training for this moment since the age of three, when she first set foot on an amateur stage. That was in Ootecamund, a suburb of Bangalore, where her father, an officer in the Indian Cavalry during the First World War, was stationed training remounts for Mesopotamia. Little Vivian Hartley (her Christian name was spelt with an 'a' until she took up acting professionally) was supposed to sing 'Little Bo-Peep' in a concert for parents and children of the regiment, all dressed up like a Dresden shepherdess. But when she got on stage she announced very firmly that she did not want to sing, but would recite it instead. And did. A child, evidently, who knew her own mind.

Apart from the remarkable determination, Vivian had, even then, a more than remarkable prettiness. She seems to have inherited her looks from both parents, that at least we can be sure of, since the pictures tell us Ernest Richard Hartley and his wife Gertrude Robinson (née Yackje) made a very handsome couple. More about them it is difficult to be sure of, since their family histories subsequently became so overlaid with myth. To overcome expected objections to casting an Englishwoman as Scarlett, Selznick announced that whereas Scarlett was the child of an Irish father and a French mother, Vivien was the child of an Irish mother and a French father. Actually both her parents came from solid, middle-class families in Bridlington, Yorkshire. Ernest's French ancestry, often invoked to explain his notorious fascination for the ladies in Calcutta and elsewhere, seems to have been remote and notional if indeed it existed at all. Gertrude's mother was apparently Irish, and she had a strict convent upbringing as a Roman Catholic which she was to hand on to her daughter, but her father, though sometimes hopefully stated to be French also, seems to have been, less romantically, of Dutch extraction.

In any case, it seems fatuously unnecessary to look for ethnic explanations of a complete original like Vivien Leigh. With her pale skin, long swanlike neck and catlike green eyes, set piquantly aslant over high cheekbones in a heart-shaped face which only emphasised the feline associations, she was never characteristic of anything but herself. We do know that her father, who went out in India in 1905 as a clerk to a brokerage firm and worked his way up to junior partner by the time he returned home in 1911 to meet and marry Vivien's mother, was, as well as being a ladies' man, dashing horseman and polo-player, a leading star of the rather grand amateur theatricals which, at the Royal Theatre, constituted most of Calcutta's English theatrical diet. He carefully destroyed all his press notices as an actor shortly after Vivien became famous in the same line, but was remembered by contemporaries as being equally at home playing upstanding heroic roles and comic or dramatic characters. Whether or not Vivien inherited her histrionic talents from him, at least this part of his life made him more immediately well-disposed to the idea of Vivien's going on the stage than was her rather narrowly religious mother.

Vivian Mary was the Hartleys' second child, and the only one to survive. She was born in Darjeeling on 5 November 1913, and was at once accounted an extraordinarily beautiful baby – as indeed she should have been according to Indian superstition, being born within sight of the peerless peak of Kanchenjunga. During her early childhood, with her father's time in the Army, they seem to have been a happy and united family. But after the war Gertrude wanted them to return to England and instead Ernest, now a senior partner in his firm, insisted that they stay on in Calcutta. Gertrude was worried about Vivian's religious education, and a strict Catholic nanny was imported from England to replace an easy-going Indian amah. Pressures of work soon forced Ernest to give up his amateur acting, but did not, apparently, inhibit his taste for romantic dalliance, so the accord between him and Gertrude was often less than complete. There is a story Vivien delighted to tell in later life (perhaps because it

At the time of the first stage appearance (aged three) reciting Little Bo Peep

indicated where some of her own character traits came from), about a dinner party organised by Gertrude in which she deliberately arranged that all the women present should be suspected liaisons of Ernest's, and all their menfolk presumably cuckolded by him. Gertrude, evidently, was not entirely without her own resources when it came to giving as bad as she got.

Fortunately, Vivian was not around them too much during this stormy passage of their marriage. In 1920 the Hartleys went home to visit, for the first time since her birth, and took her with them with the intention (Gertrude's rather than Ernest's) of finding a suitable convent boarding school in which to place her. Gertrude lighted upon the Convent of the Sacred Heart in Roehampton, then a rural backwater south-west of London. Despite Vivian's pleadings her father gave in and it was agreed that Vivian should enter the school in September, at just under seven the youngest child ever to be accepted there. It sounds like the beginning of a Dickensian tear-jerker, but oddly enough Vivian seems to have spent some of the happiest years of her life at this school. As the baby of the outfit, it is true that she was to a certain extent petted and cosseted. But on the other hand the strict discipline of the place seems to have suited her. She was actually happy to be meticulously neat and tidy, immaculately punctual, efficiently performing any task she was set and never tempted to flout the authority of the nuns – unlike her closest friend, an Irish girl some two years older than her, named Maureen O'Sullivan, who was destined to make Hollywood stardom earlier, if never on such a spectacular scale.

A garden snapshot of Vivian Hartley, aged eighteen

The girls' theatrical instincts, if any, were by no means totally stifled at Sacred Heart. They engaged in a lot of amateur theatricals and, surprisingly, dance instruction was also offered, though Vivian was the only girl to take it (from a nun who had had some ballet training before finding her vocation). This meant that displays of her class work were inevitably always solo, something which seems to have worried Vivian not at all. All testimony, in fact, indicates that she possessed remarkable poise for her age, and a curious quality of self-containment which enabled her to make friends easily, be perfectly at home with those much older than herself, and yet always remain her own prematurely private person, just as happy with her own company as with a throng of people around her. Nor did the nuns carry austerity so far as to frown on, let alone forbid, visits to the professional theatre in London. As Christmas treats the girls were taken to pantomimes and innocuous comedy shows, and one of these latter, *Round in Fifty* with George Robey at the Hippodrome, took Vivian's fancy so much that she saw it sixteen times.

She was, in fact, already settled in her own mind that she was going to be an actress. At first she thought in just a small way: maybe, she wrote to her father, if she went back to India they could act together at the Royal Theatre. He answered vaguely that that would of course be fun, but he doubted if he was likely to have much time free for acting from his busy professional life. As it was, that allowed him to come over to England only every other year to see Vivian in the summer, though Gertrude was able to come over every year. When he came they all had quiet family holidays in the west of Ireland, where he could fish (another of his manly pursuits) to his heart's content. As she grew older he continued to spoil Vivian, now with gifts of jewellery, silk stockings and Indian fabrics instead of expensive toys, and they always managed to spend some time together in London, eating out, going to the theatre she loved, and generally living, at any rate in comparison with even a rather grand convent school, something very much like the high life. All of which Vivian, early mature rather than tiresomely precocious, took in her stride.

When she was thirteen she suddenly had a lot more to take in her stride. Her parents returned to Europe for good, with quite a substantial fortune. Her father had just turned forty and her mother was still younger: they were determined to enjoy their position, and that their only child should enjoy it with them. After the quiet, sheltered years in the convent, she was suddenly taken off for four years of constant movement around Europe, from school to school and temporary home to temporary home, as her parents spent a summer in Dinard, a winter in Biarritz, and moved restlessly to Italy, Switzerland, Austria. Accordingly, Vivian found herself enrolled successively in convent schools in Dinard, where she first began to resent the strict limitations on her freedom, San Remo, where she was even the subject of complaint because of her insubordinate behaviour, and Bad Reichenhall, so that she could improve her French, her Italian (which, owing to her dislike of San Remo, she signally failed to do) and her German. Between San Remo and Bad Reichenhall she persuaded her parents to let her enrol in a secular school in Auteuil, where speech and drama were taught by an actress from the Comédie Française and she would be in easy reach of the Paris theatres. This came to a rapid end when a friend reported to her parents that she had been seen at a theatre wearing altogether too much makeup for a girl of her years, and she was promptly dragged away to the convent at Bad Reichenhall. That, however, after a few tears at being forced to relinquish Paris so abruptly, she really liked; she proved to be an excellent student of German, and laid the foundations of her considerable musical knowledge with trips to the opera in Salzburg and Vienna.

We might guess at some sort of early history like this from what we know of the mature Vivien Leigh. Her famous command of languages, her extraordinarily broad general culture, her social ease with all kinds of people – all those qualities which are supposed to be so un-English and therefore to require the postulation of exotic antecedents come into focus given this information. If she was not un-English, her upbringing certainly was. What we might not expect from the future Scarlett O'Hara, however, is her apparently submissive attitude during most of her convent schooldays, her ready (and indeed lifelong) acceptance of convent standards of personal modesty and hygiene. The brief period of rebellion at San Remo sounds a lot more in character. But on consideration, it would seem that here we have the key to many of her subsequent troubles. Without going too far into reach-me-down psychologising, it is not too difficult to guess what conflicts are likely to be set up in the child of wilful, passionate parents, born and raised in India then suddenly immersed in the order and discipline of convent life which must have represented the greatest emotional security she had ever known. Especially since in this strict community she was the petted darling, so that whatever she learned there was inculcated by kindness. In later life she was obsessive about personal neatness: she always, for example, followed the convent rule of folding the soiled garments of the day neatly and covering them from view with a specially made cloth. But of course this kind of obsessiveness can also give rise to its own contrary, when all such constraints are dramatically (and sometimes uncontrollably) thrown off. In any case, it usually suggests the presence of deep-seated guilts, the necessity to hide, even from oneself, the existence of less neat, acceptable impulses. While not everyone who has a strict Catholic education becomes a manic-depressive in later life, one cannot doubt that to one of Vivien's passionate, headstrong disposition the problem of not being at all what she ought to be, of not always reacting the way one ought to react, could set up tremors in the psyche which, denied an easy, natural outlet, become sooner or later a major earthquake which rocks and finally destroys the whole fabric.

When Vivian left school at the age of eighteen all such considerations must have seemed far away. Around puberty she had had her 'moody' phases, but that was only to be expected, and she seemed to have outgrown them. She never had any lack of attention from boys, but she seemed instinctively to know how to deal with them. Poised beyond her years, she was regarded as a model daughter, the last person to give her parents too much worry. By this time the Hartleys had come back to England, and Ernest, like many who lived off their investments, was as a result of the Depression a lot less rich than he had been. They decided to retrench a bit by taking a house near Teignmouth in the West Country for the winter. Vivian now announced as a definite, mature decision that she wished to become an actress, and her father, delighted, arranged for her to be enrolled in the Royal Academy of Dramatic Art at the earliest possible moment, which was May 1932. Meanwhile, she threw herself wholeheartedly into the social round of the country well-to-do. At a hunt ball she made a fateful encounter. It was with a thirty-one-year-old and thoroughly eligible bachelor barrister (of a local family but practising in London) called Leigh Holman. He was gentle, dreamy and handsome in a cool, fair, English sort of way. It is irresistible not to anticipate a bit and say that he was the Ashley Wilkes to her Scarlett, though of course at this point the role-models were still locked in Margaret Mitchell's imagination.

Fundamentally they were as different as chalk and cheese but therein, no doubt, lay the attraction. Certainly both were sure at once they were in love. Vivian, with the impetuosity of youth and her own character, told all her contemporaries immediately; Leigh, quieter and more circumspect, began to tell friends about six months later, with elaborate casualness, that he 'might marry Viv.' Before anything too committing could happen along those lines, however, there was her training at RADA to be embarked upon. Since her parents did not consider it a particularly good idea that she should be living alone in London, she was packed off to grandparents in Bridlington while they arranged to move into a flat in London, which would give her a sensible family base. And in May she duly embarked on the process of becoming a professional actress.

At least, that is how it looks now. Since we cannot, with hindsight, imagine Vivien Leigh as anything but an actress, we naturally assume that she had a driving ambition to be one from the first. But those who knew her at the time are by no means agreed on this. Leigh Holman certainly regarded her time at RADA as a sort of artistic finishing school, and was evidently quite surprised when she subsequently proved to be so serious about her career. Others who knew her earlier, at school, seem equally to have supposed that she had teenage fantasies because she was pretty and enjoyed attention, but would not have been surprised if she had soon forgotten all that and settled down instead to be a prominent hostess, wife and mother. No doubt at that point Vivian herself did not know exactly what she wanted and how much she wanted it.

She did well at RADA – apart from some doubts as to whether her voice was not too light and high-pitched to carry effectively in the theatre – and she played a variety of roles in school productions, including Rosalind in *As You Like It* and, less glamorously, Starveling in *A Midsummer Night's Dream*, with modest success. But in July Leigh proposed, Vivian accepted him without hesitation, and though her mother did wonder if she was sure she had enough in common with Leigh for a lifelong partnership, they certainly made a striking couple and most of their friends saw the marriage as ideal. They had a Roman Catholic marriage at the fashionable St James's, Spanish Place, on 20 December 1932, honeymooned in the Bavarian Alps, and returned in the New Year to Leigh's bachelor flat in St John's Wood. And that, but for the natural moves onward and upward in Leigh's professional career, might have been that.

Certainly Leigh thought it would be. On his urging, Vivian had left RADA before their marriage, and to all appearances she was studying only the new role of Mrs Leigh Holman – learning to entertain and be entertained, being presented in the grand manner at Court (where Queen Mary commented audibly on her extraordinary beauty), and getting pregnant. Before this last happened, though, she had managed to wheedle her way back into classes, this time not at a formal school, but with a well-known language teacher, in order to keep up her French. It was the thin end of the wedge. Once started on that, she also began general voice and movement classes. Her ambitions, if they had ever been damped down, undoubtedly rekindled, and soon she was back at RADA for another term, intending to complete a full course there. Her pregnancy changed all that. She decided to leave in June 1933, shortly after her presentation at Court and, rather improbably, a RADA performance as Shaw's St Joan, and the Holmans moved from their flat to a small house in Mayfair, which she set about furnishing and decorating with a will, first manifesting her famous flair for recognising quality in what others still regarded as junk and anticipating movements of taste in the arts by that vital two or three years which allowed style on a budget.

Her daughter Suzanne was born, a month premature, on 12 October, the occasion marked in her diary, it seems, with just the terse statement 'Had a baby – a girl.' On her return from hospital she soon found that motherhood did not make her any less restless. She threw herself even more into entertainment; she did not want to go back to RADA, but she did want to act. The following summer a chance materialised – a very small chance, it is true, to play a virtual walk-on as a schoolgirl in a Cicely Courtneidge film called *Things Are Looking Up*. It was the sort of

With her baby daughter Suzanne, 1935

The first film appearance, as a schoolgirl in Things Are Looking Up *(1934). Above: Vivien is second from the left, centre row. Gaumont British*

thing a lot of young society women did just for a lark, and were paid accordingly, at the rate of 30s a day. But Vivian took it very seriously, even suggesting that she and Leigh put off a Baltic cruise he had arranged in order that she should be ready. He put his foot down, but when she received a cable in Copenhagen that she should report on set at once she insisted on doing so. They quarrelled and Leigh completed the holiday alone. As it happened, she could have stayed on too, since a further delay meant that he was back (somewhat contrite) by the time the shooting began. To his surprise he found it was not so bad having an actress wife after all: at least she was home more, studying her role, and insisting on getting all her beauty sleep instead of her usual late nights. And since she had only one line to say, it was not exactly exhausting for either of them.

Without anyone quite recognising the fact, a career had begun. Suitably enough for an aspiring actress, Vivian soon acquired an agent (she met him at a party). He decided that first of all she needed a new professional name, and after some brain-racking they came up with 'Vivian Leigh', which was classy, easy to remember and immediately acceptable to her husband. Thus prepared, she and her agent went to see Alexander Korda, at that time the most powerful and successful film producer in Britain. He was not too encouraging: he agreed she was pretty and charming, but felt that she lacked the sort of clear, unmistakable typing which was necessary for stardom. Also, quite possibly, he felt she was too close in physical type to his own newest star creation (and loved one) Merle Oberon. Well, if she was not going to start at the top, she might as well start at the bottom, and thus thinking her agent got her the female lead in two quickies, *The Village Squire* and *Gentleman's Agreement*. Each was made in less than a week, and neither received much notice of any kind, but at least the pay was improving: for *The Village Squire* she was paid 30 guineas for six days' work. And they did get her her first professional stage work: David Horne, who had appeared in both of them, suggested her for the female lead in a play he was about to appear in, *The Green Sash*, by T. P. Wood and the improbably-named Debonnaire Sylvester.

The play ran a week at the suburban Q Theatre and then vanished without trace. It required her to wear a becoming Renaissance Florentine costume and be unjustly suspected by her elderly husband of flirting with a passing soldier. *The Times* reviewed it briefly and presciently remarked on the 'precision and lightness' of Vivian's acting, which 'should serve her well when her material is of more substance.' That was in February 1935. Immediately afterwards she was cast in her first film of any stature, *Look Up and Laugh*, in which Gracie Fields played the lead and she the ingenue. It was written by J. P. Priestley and took a whole six weeks to shoot. It was not a particularly pleasant experience, since though the star was friendly and encouraging it was directed by Basil Dean, who was notorious for bullying his

In Gentleman's Agreement *(1935).*
Paramount British

38

S·B·42·

actors and did not spare this unimportant new girl the lash of his tongue. She did not have too much time to worry about that, however, because as soon as the film was finished and before it was shown she finally got her first big break and saw her name in headlines.

The essential thing about the role in *The Mask of Virtue* was that whoever played it should be stunningly beautiful. Given that, the actress had to be able to project both innocence and experience. Carl Sternheim's play, based on the same incident from Diderot as Robert Bresson's film *Les Dames du Bois de Boulogne*, concerns a plot by a vengeful older woman to marry off a lover who has discarded her to a prostitute masquerading as an angel of purity. The producer of the play, Sydney Carroll, took one look at Vivian and offered her the part of the girl: the fact that she could play it as well as look it seems to have been an unhoped-for bonus. Carroll, unlike Korda, was sure from the start that he was dealing with star material. He respelt her Christian name 'Vivien' (more feminine) and coached her carefully throughout rehearsals as well as watching closely over the design and the stage lighting to make the most of the way she looked.

The play opened on 15 May 1935 at the small (but undeniably West End) Ambassadors Theatre, and was an instant triumph, especially for Vivien. The first indication of this was the reaction of Korda, who was in the audience. Without waiting for the notices, he went round to her dressing-room, admitted he had made a mistake about her, and arranged to see her agent the following day to discuss a contract. The leading critics were equally enthusiastic: *The Times* commented on her ability to 'mingle very adroitly a demure repose with a lively understanding', the *News Chronicle* said she was 'an actress of uncommon gifts', and the *Manchester Guardian*, praising her acting skills, said that her future in the theatre 'should be amply secure', though it also observed a little sadly that 'when a young actress of such glamour appears we nowadays fear that the stage will at once lose her to the screen.' In other words, Vivien Leigh had very definitely arrived.

The meeting with Korda resulted in a five-year contract and in the announcement that Vivien would star first in a film of *Cyrano de Bergerac*, playing Roxanne to Charles Laughton's Cyrano. Unfortunately Laughton, not for the first or last time, created all sorts of difficulties (including forcefully expressed doubts about her casting) and the project fell by the wayside. *The Mask of Virtue* ran happily at the Ambassadors, but failed to project well when transferred to a larger theatre, went on tour and then closed. But for Vivien it had served its purpose. She was offered the lead, opposite Ivor Novello, in a stage musical by Clemence Dane and Richard Addinsell based on Max Beerbohm's story *The Happy Hypocrite*, and accepted, though the production was then postponed. More important for her private and subsequent pro-

Overnight stage star in The Mask of Virtue. *Below: with Frank Cellier*

fessional life, Vivien had met the brightest young male star of the English stage at that point, Laurence Olivier. She had first seen him on stage in 1934, and had, like half the young women in London, fallen for him completely playing the role based on John Barrymore in the satirical comedy by Edna Ferber and George S. Kaufman *The Royal Family*, called in England *Theatre Royal*. Of course, this was just a slightly more mature version of a schoolgirl crush, except that as Vivien achieved more of a position of her own in the theatre, it became more and more conceivable that something more might come of it. Olivier saw her for the first time in *The Mask of Virtue*, and was, on his side, almost equally smitten. As he recalls in his autobiography,* 'Apart from her looks, which were magical, she possessed beautiful poise; her neck looked almost too fragile to support her head and bore it with a sense of surprise, and something of the pride of the master juggler who can make a brilliant manoeuvre appear almost accidental. She also had something else: an attraction of the most perturbing nature I had ever encountered.'

In The Happy Hypocrite, *with Ivor Novello and Isabel Jeans*

With this reciprocal, though as yet unguessed attraction, something was almost bound to come of it. Shortly after *The Mask of Virtue* the Holmans met the Oliviers – at the Savoy Grill, Olivier remembers, though Vivien remembered being introduced to him and his wife there when she was dining with someone other than Leigh, and that Olivier hardly seemed to register her presence. Wherever and however, the two couples became acquainted, the Holmans visited the Oliviers for a weekend in the country, and an apparently unloaded friendship developed. But there were undertones. One day in late 1935 Vivien went alone to a matinée performance of the famous production of *Romeo and Juliet* in which Olivier and Gielgud alternated the roles of Romeo and Mercutio. It was one of Olivier's turns as Romeo, and afterwards she went round backstage to congratulate him. As she was leaving, she suddenly bent down and kissed him on the shoulder. Before the year was out they were lovers.

Olivier also became Vivien's professional mentor. On his advice she went to see Gielgud about doing the small (virtually one-scene) role of the Queen in a largely amateur production of *Richard II* he was staging in Oxford. In April 1936 *The Happy Hypocrite* finally opened, and though it got some good notices did not do well, possibly because Novello's great army of fans did not find in it the Ivor they knew and loved. As the debauched rake Lord George Hell he began in hideously grotesque makeup, and though love transfigured him along the way and he got his best notices ever as an actor, the switch was too worrying. Again, Vivien was widely appreciated, Max Beerbohm being not the least of her admirers: he said that her performance was 'of exquisite sensibility – a foreshadowing of how much may be to come in later years.' All that came for the moment was another very brief Shakespearian role, that of Anne Boleyn in *Henry VIII*, given in Regent's Park that summer under Sydney Carroll's management.

Immediately after that came the fateful moment when Olivier and Vivien were cast together. And, what was more, playing the young lovers in Korda's Elizabethan romance *Fire Over England*. Strictly speaking, it was only masterminded by Korda, who hoped it would be a new *Private Life of Henry VIII*. He kept a close parental eye on it, but handed over its realisation to German producer Erich Pommer and American director William K. Howard. Olivier and Vivien provided the fictional love interest in an otherwise reasonably factual history of the court of Elizabeth I set against the background of the Spanish Armada, and suffered from rather colourless and underwritten roles. The film was quite popular, nevertheless, owing mostly to a gallery of effective performances surrounding Flora Robson's central impersonation of the Queen. Though Korda discreetly warned Vivien and Olivier each about the other's status as a respectably and even happily married person, now they had obvious professional as well as other reasons to become inseparable. To

* *Confessions of an Actor*, Weidenfeld & Nicolson, 1982.

Fire Over England, *with Laurence Olivier. The poster* (left) *visually gives them top billing. Tunbridge/ London Films*

VIVIEN LEIGH
9054-28

complicate things, Olivier's wife, actress Jill Esmond, gave birth to a son, Tarquin, in the middle of shooting, thereby reconfirming the image of an ideal and united couple.

When the shooting was over, the Oliviers went off on an Italian holiday to recuperate, and Vivien went to Sicily with an old friend of Leigh's when Leigh at the last moment could not go with her. Somehow the two couples met up in Capri and though, as they used to say in Doris Day movies, NOTHING HAPPENED there, in fact it seems to have been the point of no return for the Vivien/Olivier relationship. From then on it was inevitable that sooner or later they would both have to ask for divorces so as to be able to marry each other. Jill Esmond, it seems, guessed at the truth some time before any disclosures were officially made, but Leigh seems to have been still taken by surprise when, after what Olivier describes as 'Two years of furtive life, lying life. Sneaky,' Vivien finally wrote from Denmark, where they were appearing together in *Hamlet*, to tell him she was leaving him.

The young sophisticate in Dark Journey. *Tunbridge/London Films. Below:* with Conrad Veidt. *Tunbridge/London Films*

The secret romance with Olivier undoubtedly occupied much of Vivien's spare time and energy during 1936 and 1937, but she was kept busy on her own account too. Right after *Fire over England* she went into two films produced and directed for Korda's London Films by Victor Saville, both of which, if scaling no heights, showed her off to good effect in female leads. The first was *Dark Journey*, an intricate spy story in which she and Conrad Veidt were cast as double agents on opposite sides during the First World War who fall in love and after a series of increasingly complex revelations (Vivien is a couturier who smuggles secrets recorded in the embroidery of her dresses) end up somewhere in the middle. No one quite understood the story, but the public liked it, and Vivien looked very pretty indeed. The second, *Storm in a Teacup*, was based on a comedy by James Bridie about goings-on in a Scottish village and co-starred another relative newcomer, Rex Harrison. It was widely hailed as a new breath of reality in the British cinema, and Vivien again got favourably

In Storm in a Teacup. *London Films*

Above: *with Michael Shepley in* Bats in the Belfry

noticed. Between the two films she did two short-lived stage comedies, *Because We Must* in February 1937 and *Bats in the Belfry* in March – all while Olivier was staking one of his major claims to fame in the uncut *Hamlet* directed by Tyrone Guthrie at the Old Vic, which Vivien managed to see fourteen times. It was while she was rehearsing for *Because We Must* that Vivien read the new bestseller *Gone With the Wind*, and immediately saw herself as Scarlett, giving all the cast copies of the book on opening night and urging her agent to propose her for the role to Selznick. Selznick showed little interest, though he promised to look at *Fire Over England* to see if Vivien had any useful qualities (presumably he thought she did not).

Then in June Olivier was asked to take his *Hamlet* to Elsinore, Denmark, and asked Vivien to play Ophelia there with him. They were at the time appearing together in a rather ill-fated film called *Twenty-One Days*, scripted by Graham Greene from a short story by John Galsworthy, produced (and liberally interfered with) by Korda, and directed by Vivien's *bête noire* Basil Dean, who had got on scarcely better with Olivier in two earlier stage productions. Korda rearranged the shooting schedule so that his stars could go off to Elsinore for a week in the middle, then took over himself, shot additional sequences and edited it to his own

Twenty-One Days. Right: *with Laurence Olivier.* Below: *on location with sundry cockney characters.* London Films

49

Titania in the Old Vic Midsummer Night's Dream, *1937*

satisfaction as a star-building vehicle. Or possibly not so much to his own satisfaction, since he shelved it for two years unseen, only to sell it to Columbia, who held it for another year before releasing it in January 1940, hoping to cash in on the new Hollywood eminence of its two stars. The *Hamlet* was a much more satisfactory experience, getting Vivien her first rave notices in a classic and decisively cementing the bond between her and Olivier, so that when they got home to London they moved out from their respective spouses and into a new house together in Chelsea. Vivien ended the year by making her own first appearance at the Old Vic, playing Titania in Tyrone Guthrie's very successful production of *A Midsummer Night's Dream*, exquisitely dressed by Oliver Messel and with Robert Helpmann, who rapidly became a close friend, as Oberon.

By now things were really taking off, and Vivien's two films of 1938 were both, in their different ways, significant moves forward for her. *A Yank at Oxford* was the first film of an ambitious new programme of British production instituted by MGM, and so guaranteed her more exposure in America than she had ever received before. The 'Yank' was Robert Taylor, and his true love

A Yank at Oxford. Below: *undergraduate hero (Robert Taylor) and university siren*. Right: *Vivien and Maureen O'Sullivan – schoolfriends reunited on set.* Davis Boulton/MGM

was played by Maureen O'Sullivan, Vivien's old convent school-friend, now established as a minor-league Hollywood star. Vivien played a shorter role as the local vamp ('I love to help the undergraduates. Especially the new ones') but it was more showy that the nominal heroine's, and though in some scenes she is visibly uncertain with the degree of worldliness she has to assume, she is still the most memorable thing around. In *St Martin's Lane*, called in the States *Sidewalks of London*, Charles Laughton plays a London busker and Vivien the thieving waif he puts into his act and finally sees become a great star. Neither of them is, truth to tell, particularly good, though the actual busking is quite amusing, albeit improbable, in a RADA end-of-term romp sort of way. And the film did get widely shown in the States, and better liked if anything than in England, where its cute-Cockney falsities were more evident.

With Rex Harrison in St Martin's Lane. *Mayflower Pictures/Associated British*

St Martin's Lane: *birthday in a garret, on the eve of discovery; with Charles Laughton and* (above) *Rex Harrison with notepad. Mayflower Pictures/Associated British*

So, what next? Everyone agreed Vivien was a beauty and had enormous charm and personality. Olivier, with a partial but not totally unrealistic lover's eye, felt that she was much more: that with the right training and experience she could be a great classical actress. She, admiring him beyond bounds, wanted to be what he thought she could be and believed she could eventually stand worthily beside him. Others felt the same, or at least accepted that she had a comparable, if dangerously different, talent. Not everyone agreed. Michel Saint-Denis, it may be recalled, refused outright to consider her as even a serious possibility in Chekhov. It is difficult to guess exactly where she would have gone next if Olivier had decided to stay firmly in London and perform only grand classical roles, instead of taking another chance on Hollywood with *Wuthering Heights*. Somehow her casting in *Gone With the Wind* seems so inevitable that one wonders if her determination might not have carried her through even without Olivier's presence as an added spur. Mercifully, all speculation apart, what happened to Vivien Leigh in 1939 has long passed into film history.

The Ideal Couple

I T IS an old Hollywood superstition that an Oscar jinxes a career. Almost as old as the coexistent superstition that no star ever gets anywhere without one. Both are demonstrably untrue, as a trail of much-honoured yet indestructible stars and of stars of first importance who never got a nod from the Academy will bear witness. But it is certainly true that success is sometimes more difficult to survive than failure. Even before Vivien Leigh duly picked up her Oscar for *Gone With the Wind*, the film and her performance in it were evidently the wonder of the age. The eight Oscars the film received (plus a special award and the Irving Thalberg Award for its producer David O. Selznick) were just a somewhat belated confirmation of what everybody already knew anyway. And with or without an Oscar, Vivien had the same problem: having just starred in her first Hollywood film and found that it went right on to become the most successful film in the history of the cinema might well have stopped her dead in her tracks, intimidated by the impossibility of finding an encore to top it.

Not Vivien, though. She seems to have acted throughout with an almost preternatural calm and confidence. Partly, no doubt, it was because she had a very clear sense of her own destiny, which had not yet let her down. She had been convinced that she would be taken up by Korda, the great British star-maker, and time had proved her right. She was sure from the first that she was right for Scarlett O'Hara, and again had carried all before her. When she had barely met Laurence Olivier, the most exciting man on the British stage, she had confided to a friend her firm intention of marrying him: now the obvious obstacles (like his wife and her husband) were in the process of being removed and that particular prize too was within her grasp. Clearly, she could afford to be calm and confident. True, she did from time to time have brief fits of 'restlessness', but then that was no doubt all part of the artistic temperament, nothing, surely, to worry about.

She did not manage to get her own way in everything, of course, but the failures were easily bearable. She wanted very much to star with Olivier in a film, but for the moment that was not to be. She could certainly contrive to be philosophical about not being cast opposite him in *Rebecca* since she was intelligent enough to know that the role was not really suitable for her, however much she might fight against the idea. She was more irritated that he had not been put opposite her in her next film, *Waterloo Bridge*, though it was clearly no more than an insubstantial tear-jerker about a dancer who takes to prostitution when she believes her lover has been killed in the First World War, only to recognise him later and kill herself after finding she cannot forget the past in his stately Scottish home. Originally the idea had been to cast Olivier as the Scottish laird who loves her, but in the event the role went to Metro's own star Robert Taylor, and Vivien, being lent out by Selznick, had no say in the matter.

Still, Olivier was near at hand, going straight from *Rebecca* to

Willinger portrait in ballet costume for Waterloo Bridge. *MGM*

Pride and Prejudice, also at MGM (Vivien thought she should be playing Elizabeth Bennett to his Mr Darcy, but Metro again preferred their own new contract star, Greer Garson). And in January 1940 the Oliviers' divorce came through (Jill naming Vivien as co-respondent), followed three weeks later by the Holmans' (Leigh naming Olivier as co-respondent). Though the divorces did not become final for six months, so that Vivien and Olivier could not marry immediately, at least there was now no need for secrecy (or indeed possibility of it) about their relationship, so they moved in together next door to Olivier's close friend Ronald Colman and his wife. The only real cloud on the horizon was the war in Europe. Both of them wanted to return to England as quickly as possible, but both had contractual obligations in America, and the British government, through the British Ambassador, was urging Britons in Hollywood to stay put, in the belief that they would be helping the war effort more by their public visibility than they would be able to back in a beleaguered Britain.

To employ their time to best effect, and hopefully to make a lot of money, they planned a return to the stage together, and what would seem to be a more suitable vehicle for the two most famous real-life lovers in the world than *Romeo and Juliet*? The suggestion came originally from Vivien's friend and confidant George Cukor, though he was later one of the first to see (in Chicago, where he picked the show up on its pre-Broadway tour) that the enterprise was fated. Quite why is more difficult to establish. You would think that the formula could not go wrong, even if the production was in some way lacking. Reviews and eye-witnesses remark on evident technical problems, mostly arising from the use of an elaborate revolving-stage setting which was meant to keep the action flowing swiftly from scene to scene but in fact tended to go wrong, not fit on to the stage of the various theatres the production visited on its way to New York, and be so noisy as to drown vital sections of dialogue. But still, what about all the publicity and assured box-office appeal of the stars? Ideas based on that involved, it seems, a fatal confusion of two distinct audiences. Many of the millions who flocked to see them in movies would not dream of going to see them appearing live in some probably boring and incomprehensible classic on stage, while their imposing record of stage performances in England, and even a recent major success for Olivier on Broadway, were apparently invalidated for snooty New York theatre critics and theatregoers by their enormous recent successes as film stars. The general tone of the Broadway reviews, in fact, was slightly patronising, as though these Hollywood vulgarians were being ticked off for their presumption in tackling the Bard in a live theatre.

This was all particularly trying in that Vivien and Olivier had invested their combined savings of some $40,000 in the show, and saw it all vanish – indeed, during the month it struggled on in New York, they were losing $5000 a week just keeping the

Waterloo Bridge. Above: *the bad news arrives*. Below: *dancer and laird (Robert Taylor). MGM*

Above: *the young lovers on stage as Romeo and Juliet*. Left: *a joint portrait by Laszlo Willinger*

gigantic 51st Street Theatre open. Ironically, in the light of Vivien's constantly recurring sense of inferiority to Olivier in classical roles, she in general got better reviews for her Juliet than he did for his Romeo, but in a commercial disaster of such magnitude the point was academic. In the circumstances, it was no doubt pardonable that nerves might get more than usually frayed, but even so, there were in Vivien's behaviour at this time what one may with hindsight see as disturbing signs. The English actor Jack Merivale, later to become a very important figure in Vivien's life but at this time merely a minor member of the company (playing Balthasar) and Olivier's understudy, recalls one weekend invitation to Katherine Cornell's house outside New York, borrowed for the duration by Vivien and Olivier, which ended very uncomfortably. They had stayed on in the East after *Romeo and Juliet* closed; and after Merivale had done a couple of weeks in another play he came to visit. Things went smoothly at first, then one evening Vivien began to behave more and more bizarrely; she became first very vague and inattentive, then suddenly switched to an outburst of hysterical and totally ir-rational fury, set off by a game of Chinese chequers, which ended with her accusing him of trying to come between her and Olivier and virtually ordering him out of the house.

At this period such an outburst was an apparently isolated incident, which seemed so unlike the way Vivien normally behaved that those around her dismissed it from their minds, putting it down, perhaps, to her inability to handle drink in any quantity. A little later, when it was discovered she was suffering from tuberculosis, similar bouts of 'nerves' were written off as side-effects of her physical condition. It was more than a decade later that Laurence Olivier, the one most intimately, frequently and painfully involved, finally faced the fact that she was suffering from a serious psychological disturbance – was indeed incurably a victim of manic-depressive cycles which could make her a stranger, and at times a very hostile stranger, to her nearest and dearest.

Though incidents like that with Jack Merivale at Sneden's Landing were in the nature of an advance warning, for the moment everything was going as smoothly as could be expected. Their financial situation was decidedly touchy, and their recent misfortune as Romeo and Juliet did not encourage backers for such comparable ventures as a stage production of *Antony and Cleopatra* starring them. On the other hand, neither was lacking in offers to appear on stage, separately or together, in things less grand than Shakespeare, and Hollywood was likely to welcome them with open arms whenever they chose to return. At this time they were particularly in need of some extra money as they wanted to bring over to America their respective children, away from the blitz, even if their own prime impulse was still to return to Britain themselves and do what they could for the war effort. Vivien was offered a Broadway role she really wanted to take, in the Theatre Guild production of *Marie Adelaide*, which had already been offered unsuccessfully to Ingrid Bergman. In Vivien's case, as in Ingrid's, Selznick put his foot down, reminding her of contract obligations and of his generosity (as he saw it) in allowing her, against his better judgment, to do *Romeo and Juliet* when logically she should have been working for him in some sort of follow-up to her *Gone With the Wind* success. Not, as it happened, that he had anything specific in mind for her, but the message was clear: return to Hollywood or else.

At this moment the other producer Vivien still had some sort of contractual obligation to, Alexander Korda, reappeared on the scene, but this time in the role of something very like a saviour. Since the beginning of the war in Europe, Korda had been going to and fro between London and Hollywood, arranging (to a large extent on direct orders from his personal friend Winston Churchill) to complete in America his stimied English production *The Thief of Bagdad* and produce a series of 'British productions abroad', with at least one eye on the value of these as propaganda for Britain in the still neutral USA. Since the Neutrality Act forbade direct propaganda, these had to be apparently simple entertainment films which indirectly glorified the values of British culture and the British way of life. No one could object to his planned

Back in Hollywood after the honeymoon

version of Kipling's *Jungle Book*, for instance, as violating the act. His latest project, however, was a little more suspicious. He wanted to do a dramatisation of the love affair between Britain's naval hero Lord Nelson and Lady Hamilton, and wanted Olivier and Vivien to play the leads.

Suspect under the Neutrality Act or no, the project was the answer to their prayers. They could star together in good, meaty, popular roles, and Selznick, because of his original agreement with Korda for Vivien's services, was in no position to object. Moreover, this was undoubtedly something they could do for the war effort; the historical parallel between a Britain beleaguered in the Napoleonic Wars and Britain now beleaguered in Hitler's war was clear enough not to need emphasising, and Nelson's victory at Trafalgar provided an impeccably historical chance to wave the British flag. And, vital for their immediate situation, Korda offered to pay half their salaries in advance, so that they could bring over Olivier's son accompanied by his almost ex-wife, and Vivien's daughter accompanied by her mother. This was accomplished as quickly as possible, and in July 1940 they returned to Hollywood to prepare for the start of production in October.

Before that, of course, there was one little formality. Vivien's divorce from Leigh and Olivier's from Jill both became final in August. They could at last marry, but how to do it without a blaze of publicity? Ronald Colman and his wife Benita Hume had the answer to that one: they should drive up to Santa Barbara, quietly register with the County Clerk there and then, after the three days required for the licence to be valid, get married in a completely private ceremony in the house of some close friends living nearby at one minute past midnight on 31 August, and hop immediately on to the Colmans' yacht, moored in Santa Barbara, for a short honeymoon, thereby presenting the world with a *fait accompli*. Everything went according to plan, and when they were next seen in Hollywood they were what they were to be called for the next twenty years: the Oliviers.

The Oliviers were soon at work on their first, and surprisingly enough their last, major starring film vehicle together, *Lady Hamilton*, known in America as *That Hamilton Woman! Fire over England* had in effect started their romance and *Twenty-One Days* had tried, ineffectually, to exploit it, but *Lady Hamilton* was the first time that this real-life ideal couple had been showcased together, and the chemistry between them on screen was so striking that one can only be amazed no further use was made of it: a matter of timing, no doubt, and fate, that all further attempts to reunite them on screen failed. Thus *Lady Hamilton* remains a unique document. Though it was made quickly and on the cheap (not only black and white, which was normal at the time, but using a lot of model shots and mock-ups instead of location shooting and elaborately finished sets), it still catches the excitement of two of the most beautiful people in the world, made more

Gone With the Wind. Previous
page: *as Scarlett O'Hara.* Right: *the
poster.* Below: *Scarlett off-duty, with
a most unhistorical cigarette.* MGM

Left: *the poster for* That Hamilton Woman! *UA.* Below: *Ronald Searle's composite portrait of the Oliviers as reigning monarchs of the London stage*

ALEXANDER KORDA
presents
Vivien *Laurence*
LEIGH ★ OLIVIER in
THAT
HAMILTON WOMAN!
with ALAN MOWBRAY · GLADYS COOPER
SARA ALLGOOD · HENRY WILCOXON
Released thru UNITED ARTISTS

VIVIEN LEIGH

Vivien Leigh in 1936

Below: *for the film* Caesar and Cleopatra.
Wilfred Newton/J Arthur Rank

Opposite: *with Laurence Olivier in*
Romeo and Juliet

Above left: *with Laurence Olivier in* The School for Scandal. Right: *the showgirl without her prince in* The Sleeping Prince

Left: *with Laurence Olivier, setting off homeward after completing the film of* A Streetcar Named Desire. *Bert Six/Warner Bros*

Opposite: *portrait at the time of* A Streetcar Named Desire. *Warner Bros*

Overleaf: *portrait at the time of* The Deep Blue Sea. *Ted Reed/20th Century Fox/London Films*

beautiful by their proximity to each other, and two famous lovers of history played by two famous lovers in life.

Otherwise, R. C. Sherriff's script plumbs no great depths, and Nelson remains a stock heroic figure rather than the complex, tormented person he actually was. Lady Hamilton was regarded, at her peak, as one of the great beauties of her day, much painted and adored by the cognoscenti for her rather absurd-sounding *poses plastiques*. In the film she is just as beautiful, and quite a bit more refined – for by the time of her liaison with Nelson she was already noticeably coarsened and blowsy, as depicted in Rattigan's somewhat more realistic play, *A Bequest to the Nation*. True, Korda did feel himself compelled by the Production Code to put in not only a scene in which Nelson acknowledged to his clergyman father that his relationship with Emma was wrong though he was too weak to resist it, but also a prologue showing Emma thrown into jail in Calais, old, drunken and impoverished. However, when he was able he removed both these excrescences, and most of the copies of the film now in circulation are without them, so we are left with just the romance and nothing else.

The film had a large and deserved success, particularly in Britain, where it immediately became one of Churchill's favourite films. More improbably, it was shown in Russia while friendship among the Allies was at its warmest, and became one of Stalin's favourite films also. And a story, possibly apocryphal, that a captured copy was seen several times and warmly approved by Hitler adds the finishing touch. In America the film's success was not quite so spectacular, but still more than decent, and though later on in 1941 it was one of the principal films by British emigrés (along with Chaplin's *The Great Dictator* and Hitchcock's *Foreign Correspondent*) to come under close scrutiny by a Senate Committee investigating the neutrality of Hollywood film-makers, the storm blew over when Japan attacked the States at Pearl Harbour in December 1941 and America finally entered the war. So the Oliviers, in making it, could very definitely feel they were doing something to help the British war effort as well as doing their professional careers good. Meanwhile Laurence Olivier went ahead quietly training and getting himself a flying licence, since that would constitute the sort of specialist qualification needed to get him, as he wished, into the Fleet Air Arm back home in Britain. Thus equipped, in December 1940, and brushing aside all arguments, they set sail for Lisbon after Vivien had bidden Suzanne a fraught farewell in Vancouver, complicated by baseless rumours of a kidnapping plot. From Lisbon they flew to Bristol to arrive in the middle of an air-raid. They were well and truly home.

In Britain things at once began moving for Olivier. He got himself accepted for service and played an episodic role in *Forty-Ninth Parallel* before he was needed. Vivien was more at a loose end and she did not manage, as she had hoped, to get into the Old Vic company for that season. A revue touring airfields,

That Hamilton Woman! Opposite: *in all her glory.* Left: *with Nelson (Laurence Olivier).* Below left: *old and forgotten.* Below: *a break in the shooting. Robert Coburn/UA*

though it was with Olivier as well as John Clements and Constance Cummings, was not much compensation. An enquiry from the Theatre Guild in New York as to whether she would consider playing in Shaw's *Caesar and Cleopatra* for them did not seem to be much help either, since having fought so hard to come back to Britain with Olivier a return to America was the last thing she would contemplate. But at least it turned her thoughts in a new direction. She would like to play Shaw's Cleopatra, and with a film already in the planning stage by Gabriel Pascal, the unpredictable Hungarian who had talked Shaw round into letting his plays be filmed, there seemed to be every chance she might. But meanwhile, what about another Shaw play to work her way in and help convince Shaw, if convincing were needed, that she would be the right choice for the film?

After some thought and reading, Olivier suggested *The Doctor's Dilemma*, with its one female role, that of Jennifer Dubedat, wife of the brilliant but impossible artist Louis Dubedat, who is finally required to acquiesce in his medical murder. It is not one of Shaw's easier roles, as he had himself warned an earlier actress to play it, Lillah McCarthy. The character is hardly sympathetic, and depends a lot on the given charms of the actress to flesh out its rather colourless writing. However, it was a challenge, the play itself was good, and she would have a chance to wear some very becoming Edwardian clothes. So with the enthusiastic support of Binkie Beaumont of the H. M. Tennant management the project was set in motion. First a six-month tour round the regional centres, then a glamorous run at the Haymarket, long a London home of well-upholstered classic productions.

The tour was so arranged, taking in Aberdeen, Edinburgh, Glasgow, Manchester, Leicester, Leeds and Derby, that Vivien could often commute, at least for the weekends, to the Oliviers' new home at Worthy Down, near the airfield where Olivier was stationed. The play was a great success in what people were then not too self-conscious to call the provinces. The elegant settings by Michael Relph and graceful costumes by Sophia Harris brought a welcome touch of escapist grace and colour to the drab wartime stage. Also, Vivien was ideally suited to the task of making Jennifer attractive with the relatively little help Shaw had given her. Cyril Cusack was playing Dubedat well, but with perhaps insufficient charm to take the edge off the character's monstrosity as a human being. A couple of weeks after the London opening on 4 March 1942, Cusack was taken ill in the middle of a performance,

As Jennifer Dubedat in The Doctor's Dilemma *– Shaw's favourite photograph*

so his understudy took over until he could be properly replaced by Peter Glenville, better known subsequently as a director than as an actor. Glenville played the role for some months, but then he too collapsed, with jaundice, and was replaced by his understudy. But for once this string of misfortunes brought playgoers – and Vivien – an unexpected bonus. The following Monday the audience was surprised and delighted to find none other than John Gielgud playing opposite her. Apparently Dubedat was one of the only two Shaw roles he had ever wanted to play, and as the opportunity was there and he was free, he had promptly proposed himself and learnt the part over the weekend.

In all, *The Doctor's Dilemma* ran thirteen months at the Haymarket – a record for any Shaw play. During the run, Vivien got her first opportunity to meet Shaw. Though he was in London, he had made it a rule never to go to any productions of his plays, but since Pascal was eager to cast her in *Caesar and Cleopatra* he was curious to meet her, and she was summoned to his flat in Whitehall Court. Determined to make a good impression, she stage-managed her visit to perfection. Binkie Beaumont went along with her, and she tactfully kept the conversation on general lines, letting her natural charm and wit do their work, with never the slightest mention of Cleopatra. Shaw obviously knew exactly what was going on but as ever appreciated a display of consummate technique, and late in the interview suddenly said as though the idea had just struck him, 'You know, what you ought to do is play Cleopatra!' When Vivien playfully demurred he was quick to reply in kind 'You'd *look* wonderful. You don't need to be an actress – the part's fool-proof.' And as she left he added 'You are the Mrs Pat Campbell of the age' – a two-edged compliment, but at least a tribute to her beauty, charm, and skill in getting her own way.

So, the role of Cleopatra was hers, but Pascal would not be able to start shooting for several months after *The Doctor's Dilemma* closed. Olivier, meanwhile, had appeared in the pro-Soviet propaganda film *Demi-Paradise*, and planned a major film of Shakespeare's *Henry V*, which he would produce and direct as well as star in. He automatically assumed that Vivien would play the small role of Katherine, whom Henry courts and marries: they had in fact been playing the light-hearted courtship scene together in the touring Air Force revue. But here Selznick unexpectedly put his foot down. Vivien had been rebellious enough over her contract, and flatly refused to go back to Hollywood for any of the roles he had offered her, including a *Jane Eyre* cunningly sweetened with the suggestion that her daughter Suzanne might be cast as Jane when a child. But now he was adamant: it was before the convention had been established of important stars playing guest roles in prestigious productions or just for fun, and he felt that Scarlett O'Hara could not possibly return to the screen in a role which consisted of just two scenes. Disappointed, Olivier was forced to cast another young actress in the role, and

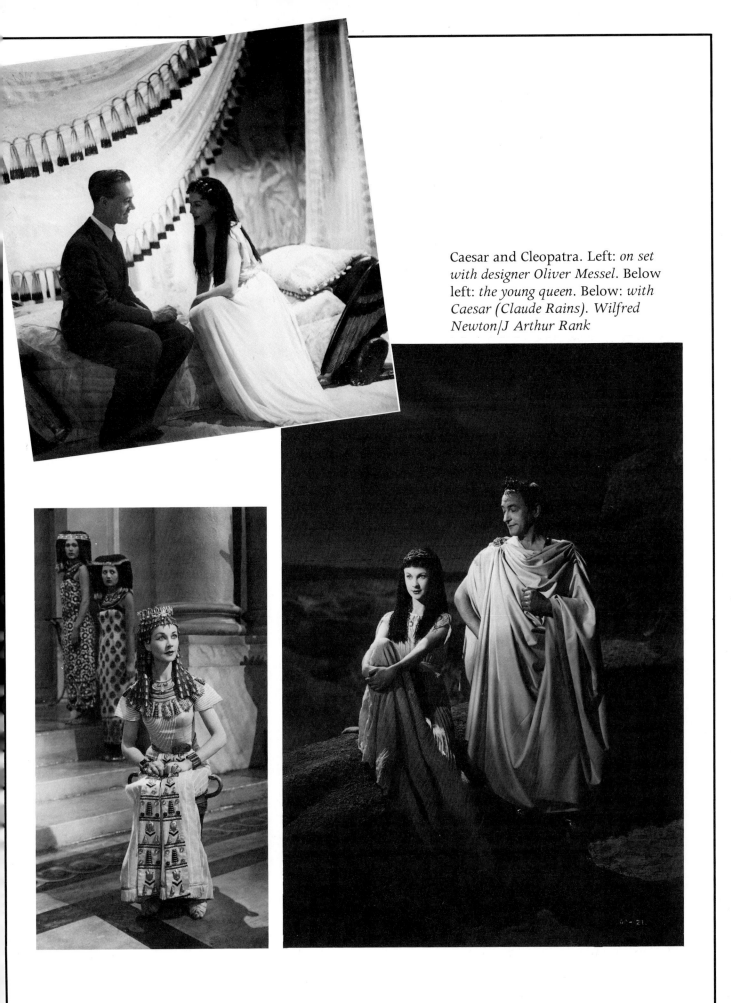

Caesar and Cleopatra. Left: *on set with designer Oliver Messel*. Below left: *the young queen*. Below: *with Caesar (Claude Rains)*. *Wilfred Newton/J Arthur Rank*

Vivien occupied her spare time before *Caesar and Cleopatra* by carrying out every actor's wartime obligation to give up six weeks a year to ENSA or CEMA entertaining the troops or keeping the home fires burning in factories and other places where war-workers were far from the usual entertainments. This time Vivien's involvement was with another scratch revue, *Spring Party*, in which she toured North Africa for six weeks looking decorative and diverting the Eighth Army with a couple of poems and a song parodying her Scarlett O'Hara persona. (It is recorded that during a preliminary discussion of what she should do in the show, she suggested the potion scene from *Romeo and Juliet* and John Gielgud, with his famous lack of tact, cheerfully replied, 'Oh no, Vivien; only a great actress can do that sort of thing!') Others in the show included Bea Lillie, Leslie Henson and Dorothy Dickson, and the schedule was gruelling, but at least the sun and dryness seemed to help a rather worrying cough she had recently developed.

Back in England she still had time to spare before *Caesar and Cleopatra*, in fact almost a year. She seems to have done nothing in that time except, presumably, be Mrs Laurence Olivier. But for once she did not chafe too much while Pascal was searching Hollywood for her leading man. Eventually, around May 1944 she found that she was pregnant, and it was all she could do to persuade her doctor that she should make the film at all. Finally shooting started on 12 July 1944, a week after the D-Day landings in Normandy. Oddly, though it seemed to be a project everyone was enthusiastic about, *Caesar and Cleopatra* did not turn out to be a happy production. Shaw, knowing Pascal of old, predicted (correctly) that it would go way over budget, and in fact the cost escalated from under half a million pounds to over a million and a quarter, making it the most expensive British film ever up to that time. Pascal had the temperament of a perfectionist, but unfortunately no matching talent. The shooting dragged on and on with no palpable result, and the finished film everywhere lacked the lightness essential to this whimsical comedy. Worse, about six weeks into shooting Vivien had a miscarriage and lost the baby she had so longed for. Tragic as this was for her, it was hardly any less disturbing for the film. At the start she allegedly assured everyone she was not pregnant. After she 'discovered' that she was, all her scenes had to be shot first, before the pregnancy began to show, and then her miscarriage delayed everything for months and enforced another rearrangement of the schedule. When she returned to the studio the film had ground on into November. Even after she had finished shooting her role it continued, with expensive, uncomfortable and unnecessary location shooting, well into 1945, and did not finally have its première until December of that year.

At least, the making of *Caesar and Cleopatra* brought Vivien further contact with Shaw, which on the whole they both seem to have enjoyed, even though he privately growled to Pascal about her diction and wondered if he would personally have to take over and correct it. (Bizarre thought!) She also received two of the inimitable Shaw postcards. He first wrote:

Your Claudius (sic) Caesar is not rather thin and stringy (I have just seen him); so will you say instead: 'You are hundreds of years old; but you have a nice voice, etc.'
I think this is the only personal remark that needs altering; but if there is anything let me know.
G.B.S.

When Vivien replied (from the studio) that she was sure she could make audiences see Claude Rains as thin and stringy by the way she said the line, a rebuke was not slow in coming:

No, Rains is not stringy, and would strongly resent any deliberate attempt to make him appear so. Besides 'You are hundreds of years old' is a much better line, as it belongs to the childishness of Cleopatra in the first half of the play.
I never change a line except for the better.
Don't be an idiot.
G.B.S
Why don't you put your address in your letters?

But all in all Vivien was glad when her part in the shooting was over, and had already premonitions of the critical drubbing that awaited everything in the film except her. Indeed, it is a thousand pities the rest of the film is so leaden, over-designed and under-directed, for Vivien's Cleopatra is one of her most enchanting creations, a kitten you know at once is going to grow up into a very formidable cat. In fact, she is as near perfection in the role of Shaw's Cleopatra as one can well conceive, though this seems to have been fully realised only when, a few years later, she finally played the part on stage and the unfortunate surroundings of the film were all but forgotten.

Apparently it was almost immediately after she had completed work on *Caesar and Cleopatra* that it became evident there was something seriously wrong with her health. At first it seemed that it was primarily or wholly psychological. First she went through a prolonged bout of depression, which might well have been a delayed reaction to the long and disheartening shooting as well as to the miscarriage. Then one night she scared the daylights out of Olivier by having her most pronounced bout of sheer hysteria yet, abusing and even physically attacking him for no apparent reason. Afterwards she was as mystified as he was, and deeply contrite. So maybe she had just drunk a little too much . . . In any case, there was another work project on the horizon. Olivier had been sent and read Thornton Wilder's historical comic-strip of a play *The Skin of Our Teeth*, in which Tallulah Bankhead was having an enormous success on Broadway. He thought the role of Sabina, the resourceful ever-feminine

Sabina, woman through the ages in
The Skin of Our Teeth

woman who survives everything from the beginning of time would be ideal for Vivien, and when she read it she thought the same – particularly if he would direct her.

He would, of course, and there was no difficulty finding a production set-up or a theatre. There was one little difficulty, though: Selznick. He had been rumbling on ever since Vivien had returned to England about her going back to Hollywood to fulfil the terms of her contract. She had politely but persistently refused. After all, he had been well recompensed for her services by both Korda and Rank in the two films she had made since *Gone With the Wind*, and Selznick was at this time scarcely involved in production at all himself, so it would be just a matter of his selling her to whomever he chose rather than directly guiding her career or letting her choose. But when it was announced that she was to appear in *The Skin of Our Teeth* in London he at once tried to get an injunction preventing her. Vivien's reply was (a little improbably) that since she was British she might always be drafted into a factory to do war-work if she did not continue to do her own job, i.e. act on the British stage. At any rate, the argument was good enough for an English court. Selznick lost his case, and that was the effective end of an arrangement which had been virtually a dead letter from the start. In anticipation of such a verdict *The Skin of Our Teeth* had been rehearsing in London, and was able to open on schedule in Edinburgh in April 1945.

Meanwhile, early in the year, something happened which had far-reaching consequences. Olivier found, fell in love with, and insisted on buying an at least semi-stately home, a house called Notley Abbey, near Thame, which went back, in parts, to the thirteenth century. It was, when he found it, something of a wreck, and Vivien was dead set against it. But such was Olivier's enthusiasm that she let herself be overruled and the place was bought, though in the middle of winter with burst waterpipes and the like it was barely habitable. By this time she was well embarked on rehearsals for *The Skin of Our Teeth*, after which came the tour of seven cities and the West End opening on 15 May – this last enlivened by a sharp exchange, coming glancingly to blows, between irate director Laurence Olivier and apparently unrepentant latecoming critic James Agate, though in his review he made ample amends by describing Vivien, in one of her favourite phrases, as 'half dabchick and half dragonfly.' But then, nearly all the London notices were ecstatic, about Vivien and even about the play, though many playgoers seemed to have difficulty in understanding it. It looked set for a long, safe run, and Olivier went off on tour with the Old Vic Company playing to the troops in Germany. But some eight weeks into the run Vivien became seriously worried about her health. The persistent cough she seemed to have got rid of in North Africa returned even more severely, and a doctor she went to in Liverpool while she was on tour recommended she have X-rays taken immediately. She delayed until London, hoping things would get better, but then she found she was constantly tired (whereas she was usually appallingly full of energy) and was losing weight for no apparent reason. She went for the X-rays, and was told that she had developed a tubercular patch on one lung. The first specialist said she should leave the play and go into hospital immediately; the second said as soon as possible, which sounded less alarming.

She did not inform Olivier of any of this, but in Hamburg he ran into a friend of the family who let slip that there was something wrong. Frantic communications and a lot of crossed wires ensued before Olivier got home and was able to sort out just how serious it was all likely to be. Vivien arranged to go into hospital for observation at the end of July, and *The Skin of Our Teeth* closed, rather prematurely, as so much of its success evidently depended on her and her newly discovered (by the public at least) sense of comedy. After six weeks of treatment the patch on her lung seemed to be under control and gradually healing, so the doctor in charge ordered her to go into a sanatorium for at least six months to complete the cure. Or tried to, but no one ever ordered Vivien to do anything. She had a morbid fear of hospitals and flatly refused. As a compromise, it was arranged that she would take six months confined to her bed at Notley, which up to then she had hardly had time even to visit. One result of this enforced stay was that she reversed her former doubts about the house, and came to love it with a fierce passion – especially when, after four months of being bedridden and constantly attended to, she was allowed to get up for short periods and could actually take more part in the decoration and furnishing, and the planting of the gardens.

In all she was confined to Notley for nine months, during which she put on weight and apparently returned to complete health. Complete physical health, at any rate, for the occasional bouts of unmotivated hysteria had continued even during her convalescence, when she could neither smoke nor drink. The scenario was generally the same: a brusque alternation of joyless, often malevolent hyperactivity and deep, totally unreachable depression. Though no one had faced up to this or quite put a name to it in Vivien's case, it was clearly a manic-depressive pattern of behaviour which was developing, and which did not seem likely to go away all of its own accord. However, once she was allowed not only up, but out, her life resumed something of its normal tenor. As it happened, Olivier was going to New York with the Old Vic and an intricate repertory of plays, including *Henry IV*, *Uncle Vanya*, *Oedipus* and *The Critic* (these last played as a double bill). Vivien was determined to go with him, and despite worries about what the excitement and the strain might do to her, the trip went off very well, even though Olivier had a painful fall during a performance of *The Critic*, injuring his leg, and there were various other upsets and narrow escapes. On the plane going back to London he was momentarily worried that she might be hysterical when she rose from her seat with a scream soon after take-off, but the worry was rapidly subsumed in a more general alarm when it was found that she had done so because one of the wings was on fire. The plane had to crash-land, but no one was hurt, and on the second attempt they reached home without further incident.

A restful summer was spent at Notley and then both the Oliviers were back in the West End, he with his triumphant *King Lear* at the New Theatre and she with a revival of *The Skin of Our Teeth* at the Piccadilly Theatre in essentially the same production as before but with a new supporting cast. A lot has been made, by way of explanation for Vivien's subsequent psychological troubles, of her growing sense of inferiority, of the disproportion between her talents and Olivier's which would forever doom her, in her own mind at least, to an inferior status – Sabina against King Lear. That may of course be true, but there is little concrete evidence for it as anything more than a hypothesis, and quite a lot of evidence which would argue against it. She seems, for example, to have enjoyed working with Olivier whenever it happened, without either desperately seeking it on all occasions or showing signs of exaggerated fear of comparison should a co-starring situation actually occur. It has even been suggested that she was bitterly disappointed when she was not invited to play Ophelia in his film version of *Hamlet*, plans for which were finished while they were on holiday together in Italy early in 1947 (she had had another bout of hysteria just before Christmas). But this too seems improbable: while she might reasonably have resented not being allowed to play Katherine in *Henry V*, a role she would have been charming and perfectly suitable in, she was certainly clear-headed enough to realise that at thirty-four she was too old to play Ophelia and too young to play Gertrude, and that anyway having Scarlett O'Hara as Ophelia, however well she played it, would certainly wreck the balance of the production.

Much more suitable, obviously, was the offer Korda made her when she got back to England: to star in a new version of *Anna Karenina*, adapted originally by Jean Anouilh and to be directed by the French (though Hollywood-experienced) director Julien Duvivier. The first essential for an Anna Karenina is to have that extraordinary quality that makes men and women stop and look at her in the street. Garbo had it, but so did Vivien, beyond a shadow of a doubt. Also, as Alan Dent, who knew Vivien very well and had at this time been working with Olivier on the script of *Hamlet*, pointed out, she was much nearer than Garbo to Tolstoy's general description of Anna: 'Anna had nothing of the *grande dame* about her, nor did she look like the mother of a boy of eight years old. By her graceful, lithe movements, the vivacious expression of her face, her eyes that changed from grave to gay so rapidly, you would have taken her for a girl of twenty. Her manner was simple and natural, yet Kitty felt that there was something about her that suggested an inaccessible world of interests, complex and poetical, and quite foreign to her own

Anna Karenina with her lover (Kieron Moore). Ted Reed/London Films

As Anna Karenina. Right: *posing for cameraman Henri Alekan.* Below: *with her husband (Ralph Richardson).* Opposite: *a radiant Anna arrives in Moscow. Ted Reed/London Films*

The Oliviers with Alexander Korda (left) *at the première of* Anna Karenina

nature and experience.' And yet the film, and Vivien's performance in it, proved by general consent a major disappointment.

The script had originally relocated the story in France, but since this was no longer to be a French production, Korda had the English translator, Guy Bolton, return it to Tolstoy's Russia. This gave every opportunity for some exquisite photographic effects – everyone remembers the snow and steam of the final scene – and dressed by Cecil Beaton, Vivien had never looked lovelier. Yet there was something missing, some vital spark which could and should have brought the character to life. It might have been something to do with the casting since her Vronsky, Kieron Moore, though handsome enough, was painfully stiff and inexperienced, and lacking in the sort of personal magnetism to which Anna could respond so passionately. But in any case, could Vivien have responded in such a way? When one thinks about it, she was always most believable depicting passions which were not primarily romantic at all (who believes that Scarlett really had more than a schoolgirl crush on Ashley, while the clash of wills with Rhett is something else again), or, later in her career, the aftermath of romantic passion in despair or late-flowering lust. It is all part and parcel of the critical distance she maintained so well in her acting and in most of the dealings of her life – she was perhaps too intelligent and too disciplined to let herself go completely in love without caring about the consequences, and her Anna is too calculated to be a toy of her own emotions. Vivien, one feels, would get everything neatly sorted out so that the social niceties could be retained even as her private passions ran their course, and seeing her in the role tends to make us uncomfortably conscious of the angle from which Anna is just a very silly woman.

The consequences of all this were more likely to be damaging in her private than in her professional life. It is impossible to think that Vivien did not have passions, and such steely control of them could not ultimately come to good. Already the surface was cracking in her short bouts of manic hysteria or her longer bouts of depression, one of which apparently engulfed most of the shooting-period. Manic-depression, as more and more authorities now seem to believe, may essentially be a physical condition, like diabetes, resulting from some chemical imbalance in the system. But if any further psychological explanation is required, it would be easy in Vivien's case to trace it back to her childhood – the heady mixture of India and Roman Catholicism – and her strict convent training, which certainly inculcated various compulsive patterns of behaviour like the instant covering of once-worn garments and the endless dabbing and spraying of scents to keep the odours of normal humanity at a safe distance. It seems that she did not suffer from extreme ups and downs when with Leigh, who never remarried and remained one of her closest, most loving friends, and we may perhaps take that as an indication that whatever her conscious mind made of her marriage to Olivier, for her unconscious mind she was still living in sin with him, and had to pay the price. As time went on the tensions this set up had to be broken more and more violently. Her unconscious drove her beyond chilling repression into a need to punish and humiliate herself in casual and most uncharacteristic sexual contacts. But for the moment, at the time of *Anna Karenina*, the disruptive forces in her psyche were held in check, although precariously, and at some cost to her abilities as an actress to identify with and make believable such characters as Tolstoy's all-for-love heroine.

This left the film beautiful but empty, with a cold and inexpressive place at its centre. Vivien quarrelled with Duvivier, snapped at Beaton and generally made trouble for everyone on set, except Korda, who assumed a sort of father-figure role and could actually control her. She did not even seem to be particularly affected, except adversely, by Olivier's being knighted in the Birthday Honours that year. But once *Anna Karenina* and *Hamlet* were completed they were able to take a prolonged family holiday together in the South of France, and Vivien's health, physical and mental, seemed to be restored. Also, they were planning to work together again in an Old Vic tour of Australia and New Zealand

Impromptu barmaid on the set of Olivier's Hamlet *on the day his knighthood was announced*

which would occupy most of 1948. The company was presenting three productions, nicely balanced between the two stars – *Richard III* for him, *The Skin of Our Teeth* for her, and *The School of Scandal* for both of them as Sir Peter and Lady Teazle. Unfortunately things started off on the wrong foot. On board ship Olivier suddenly found himself in considerable pain from the after-effects of his New York leg injury and, worse, Vivien almost at once started to show worrying signs of mania and seemed to be trying deliberately to excite his jealousy. During the long rehearsals on board ship, and the very agreeable stopover in Cape Town, both problems quietened down a bit, but there was always hanging over them both the threat of recurrence.

Professionally the tour was a triumph for both of them, taking theatre to cities in Australia, such as Perth, which had had no experience of professional acting for twelve years before their arrival. Apart from the social aspects, the trip was memorable for two things: it was halfway through it that Olivier was brusquely informed that he and Richardson had been fired from their jobs heading the Old Vic, as it was time for a change; and in Melbourne the fruitful, fateful encounter took place with a brilliant young Australian actor, Peter Finch. Finch was at that time presenting potted versions of the classics at factories during the lunch-break, and the Oliviers accepted his invitation to go and see him in *Tartuffe*. They were immensely impressed, and the eventual upshot was that Olivier put him under personal contract and

Above: *as Anouilh's Antigone at the Old Vic, with George Relph as Creon*

Right: *with Laurence Olivier in* The School for Scandal

brought him to England. Soon after that Vivien embarked on the affair which, more than anything else, brought about her ultimate separation from Olivier. It was not, apparently, the first time: Olivier in his autobiography recalls a flirtation of hers with a younger member of the touring company which was made so obvious as to become embarrassing, though whether this had any more purpose than to make him jealous was not yet clear.

Certainly Olivier was busy, preoccupied, in pain and, after a necessary operation on his knee at the end of the New Zealand visit, immobilised during the trip home. Not the most exciting or attentive of husbands, by his own admission. But it came as a complete surprise to him when, early in the Spring of 1949, Vivien suddenly announced at the lunch table that she did not love him any more – except, well, 'like a brother'. She insisted that there was no one else, but he fairly soon connected the statement with the scarcely coincidental fact that while he and she were playing a revised version of their touring repertory (Anouilh's *Antigone* in place of *The Skin of Our Teeth*) at the New Theatre, immediately back-to-back at Wyndham's his newly arrived Australian protégé Peter Finch was appearing with Edith Evans in Olivier's own production of *Daphne Laureola*. It is not quite clear when Vivien's affair with Peter Finch actually became a reality, but according to Olivier from the moment of Vivien's announcement he and Vivien lived a curiously detached life together, keeping up appearances and, as he says, despite the brother-and-sister part of it, with 'occasional acts of incest . . . not discouraged'.

The Kindness of Strangers

Professionally in 1949 both the Oliviers had more than enough to occupy their time. In Anouilh's *Antigone* Vivien showed an unsuspected range and power as a tragic actress. Although some of the critics said the usual things about her being beautiful but essentially lightweight, there was a growing regard for her serious gifts. Olivier, in his new role as a manager, was planning considerable expansion and had just taken on the lease of the St James's Theatre. And Vivien had got the bit between her teeth about another role she just had to play – Blanche Dubois in Tennessee Williams's *A Streetcar Named Desire*, which was then the sensation of the New York season with Jessica Tandy in the role. Olivier was not too happy about this and was chided by friends for his conservatism and pathetic concern for respectability. All the same, he agreed to co-produce and direct Vivien in the play, which opened at the Aldwych in October 1949.

The role proved to be, especially in the later film version, one of the twin peaks of Vivien's career, and it is the role, along with Scarlett, by which she is first and best remembered. It is surprising, bearing this in mind, that the stage presentation was by no means an unmitigated triumph, except with the paying customers, who kept it running happily for more than a year, and with professional colleagues, who appreciated her performance from a more technical point of view. Certainly from the beginning there were problems and miscalculations: Olivier was prevented from making cuts he considered necessary to speed up the play for an English audience, and forced by the Lord Chamberlain to make cuts – especially everything relating to the homosexuality of Blanche's young husband – which he believed damaged full comprehension. He also felt over-shadowed by Elia Kazan's original production to such an extent that he insisted on a credit in the programme under his name as director reading 'after the New York production'. The one major change he did make was probably a mistake: Lucinda Ballard, the New York designer, had dressed Blanche in faded finery, delicate cobwebby colours, but Williams in his stage directions indicated rather frowsty, tarty clothes, and Olivier decided to return to this, thereby helping in the misapprehension of the London critics and vocal moralists that Blanche was a prostitute and the play a lot more seamy in its subject-matter than author or cast ever intended.

All the same, Vivien was wonderfully right for the role, and in certain respects the role was all too uncomfortably right for her. In her later private life it sometimes seemed that she must be deliberately re-enacting elements of Blanche's life-story, especially in what she says about those 'many intimacies with strangers' which were 'all I seemed able to fill my empty heart with'. (Though with Vivien it was usually more like a ritual of self-degradation.) Also, the role was in some respects a natural successor to Scarlett O'Hara. Though Blanche is a much less strong character than Scarlett, she does set one wondering what happened to that kind of Southern belle with the passage of time and the decay of the

As Blanche Dubois on the London
stage in A Streetcar Named Desire,
with Bonar Colleano as Stanley

South, and Scarlett's obsession with Tara is well matched by Blanche's with Belle Reve. More specifically, what would have become of Scarlett when she had aged and her beauty faded to a degree that she could not always get her own way just by stamping her little foot? Anyway, the mastery of the Southern accent acquired for *Gone With the Wind* came in very handy, and few seem to have questioned that she was obvious casting when the film version was mooted immediately after the London production closed – as obvious as Marlon Brando, the original New York Stanley Kowalski.

For the film she went to Hollywood again, and was this time dressed by Lucinda Ballard and directed by Elia Kazan. It was nine years since she had worked there; she had made only two films during that time, when the norm for real film stars was at least two a year, so she hardly regarded herself as a film star any more, despite her Oscar. But at least this was a role she wanted, and she would be there at the same time as Olivier: he had agreed to appear in *Carrie*, based on Dreiser's gloomy novel *Sister Carrie*

and directed by William Wyler, who had previously directed him in *Wuthering Heights*. She had suffered from another serious bout of 'nerves' at the end of the London stage run of *Streetcar*, and though she seemed all right it was a worrying time while she was alone in Hollywood ahead of Olivier, who had to complete his run in Christopher Fry's *Venus Observed* at the St James's before starting out. Especially since she had well-publicised differences of opinion with Kazan over the interpretation of the role, seeing Blanche in a more sympathetic light than he did. However, once Olivier arrived, with her daughter Suzanne, now sixteen and enrolled in RADA for the autumn term, things quietened down, and after three weeks' shooting Vivien and Kazan reached a *modus vivendi*, which included her promising not to read her lines with Olivier in the evening and so be trying to follow two conflicting sets of directions. From then on shooting went more or less without a hitch, though friends thought her very tense. Things were not helped by the new status of Sir Laurence and Lady Olivier, which meant that in snobbish Hollywood they

The film of A Streetcar Named Desire. Above: *on set with Kim Hunter and Elia Kazan*. Opposite: *with Marlon Brando as Stanley. Warner Bros*

were constantly besieged with invitations and required to be the
centrepiece of pretentious parties and dinners.

Before Christmas 1950 they managed to extricate themselves
from their respective films and sail back to England (Vivien was
too nervous for the long flight). The next big question on the
agenda was, what was Olivier, what were *they*, going to do to
mark the upcoming Festival of Britain in 1951? An early suggestion
was *Caesar and Cleopatra*, which Vivien had yet to do on stage,
but as admittedly minor Shaw it seemed to lack the stature and
resonance required. The designer Roger Furse suggested, largely
in jest, that they should couple it with Shakespeare's *Antony and
Cleopatra*. Apparently no one took him seriously, possibly because
of an unvoiced doubt about Vivien's ability to play Shakespeare's
version of the character, twenty-one years older, as well as
Shaw's. But on holiday in Paris over Christmas Vivien persuaded
Olivier to think again, and soon had him convinced that the
combination, played on alternating nights, was a brilliant notion,
newsworthy as well as challenging.

So it was decided, and Vivien went into training like a prize-
fighter to lower and enrich her voice for the Shakespeare. The
two plays opened on 10 and 11 May 1951, and immediately
caused a storm of critical controversy, though as usual the
presence of both Oliviers on one stage spelt excellent box-office.
There was argument over which had the more difficult part in the

enterprise, Olivier, playing two totally different roles, Caesar and Antony, or Vivien, playing nominally the same role in two widely differing ages and styles. It was at this time that the long-lasting controversy about the rightness of the Oliviers as an acting combination first really came into the open, with many of the critics taking the view that he was being held back from full realisation of his greatness by the necessity of accommodating her and graduating his effects to match hers. The notice of the young Kenneth Tynan was particularly virulent in this respect – he worshipped Olivier and had no time at all for Vivien. Though it is clearly melodramatic to say that worries about this supposed incongruity ruined the Olivers' marriage or contributed significantly to her mental and physical breakdown, one cannot deny that it hardly made life any simpler for them, separately or together.

Again, if this was the general tone of the criticism, there were as always dissenting voices, who found Vivien's reading of Shakespeare's Cleopatra magisterial and deeply felt. (About her qualities in the Shaw there were no doubts.) Even among the initial doubters, such as *The Times*, there were often second thoughts. And in the company, it seems, if there was a question of 'taking sides' most were on Vivien's side rather than on Olivier's since he was felt to be somewhat cool and abstracted, and perhaps getting too big for his boots whereas she was enchanting. It must be admitted that sometimes there did seem to be an implied invitation to take sides since relations between the two stars appeared more strained in public than ever before. But by and large the five-month London run was very smooth and satisfactory, and Vivien did not have any more of her nasty turns.

When they took the combination of plays to New York the effect was very different. Americans responded more to the razzamatazz element in the show, the tightrope virtuosity with which the change from Shaw to Shakespeare and back again was negotiated. Also, perhaps because they were not so deeply indoc-trinated with Olivier's greatness as the London critics, the New York critics failed to see any great discrepancy between the two stars, and if anything Vivien dominated the reviews. Not that this triumph, wiping out their previous defeat with Shakespeare in New York, had any very beneficial effect. In March Vivien won her second Oscar for the film of *Streetcar*, and should have been on top of the world. But in April she had an attack of hysteria, one of the worst yet, and though she managed to continue with the plays to the end of the run, miraculously pulling herself together in company or especially on stage, Olivier succeeded in persuading her to see a psychiatrist for the first time. The visit was not a success, and was not repeated, but both of them had to face the more-than-possibility that there was something seriously psychologically wrong with her, something far beyond an occasional bad reaction to a drink too many.

'Two on the Nile'. With Laurence Olivier in (left) Antony and Cleopatra; (below) Caesar and Cleopatra

It was at this time that Vivien observed casually to an interviewer 'I'm a Scorpio, and Scorpios eat themselves out and burn themselves up like me'. Whether or not astrology had anything to do with it, she was painfully near the truth about herself. As soon as they got back to England, she went into a period of constant care by a psychiatrist and a physician – her consumption was giving cause for alarm again and she refused to take reasonable care of herself. By now, too, Olivier's feeling that he had 'lost her in Australia' had become an accepted fact of life: they remained close and kept up a façade, but he did not know what to do, and increasingly took refuge in work, work and more work, while she stayed at Notley, becoming more and more dependent on her mother and alternating long listless spells of depression with short outbursts of compulsive activity, usually occupied with cleaning and tidying and pruning to an insane pitch of intensity. The only answer, risky as it was, appeared to be more work for her, since this always brought into play again, at least for a while, her phenomenal powers of self-control. And providentially an opportunity offered: she was wanted for the female lead in a Hollywood film called *Elephant Walk*, which would begin with several weeks of location shooting in Ceylon.

Shortly before her departure, Olivier asked her who her co-star would be and she replied with extreme off-handedness 'Peter Finch'. Alexander Korda, who was present, said afterwards that it was the only really bad performance he had ever seen her give. But even if she saw the film largely as a chance to get away with her new (or perhaps by now not-so-new) lover, she had clearly reckoned without the devastating effects of shooting in Ceylon in the summer heat, not to mention the possibility that she would not get on with her director (William Dieterle) or her other co-star (Dana Andrews), with both of whom in the event she rapidly fell out. Nor, since Peter Finch's wife was along on location, can the romantic side of the proceedings have been quite as idyllic as she might have hoped. Then, in the third week of shooting, she began to show signs of a serious breakdown, hallucinating, growing confused about where she was and with whom. In desperation, Olivier was summoned by the producer and flew out from London, gravely dubious about what, if anything, he could do. In fact the only person who seemed to have any influence over her was Peter Finch, and he had despaired of keeping her calm, partly because he seemed at this time to be as passionately involved with her as she with him. Olivier appraised the situation, wished everyone luck, and returned to post-production work on his latest film, *The Beggar's Opera*, in London.

In Ceylon they somehow staggered on for the remaining week of location shooting and then moved to Hollywood for the studio scenes. Olivier, as soon as he had completed his work on *The Beggar's Opera*, went for a few days holiday to Italy with the William Waltons, but on arrival was immediately called back with the news that Vivien had suffered a complete nervous

collapse. Apparently she had become increasingly hysterical in Ceylon while shooting a scene with snakes, and had begun to get the lines of her role mixed up with those of Blanche Dubois. On the flight to California she had another bout of hysteria, tore her clothes off, tried to jump out of the plane, and had to be forcibly restrained and sedated. Despite this the decision was taken to continue shooting with her. On the first day in the studio she gave a charming, coherent interview to Louella Parsons, but then had an intense attack of hysteria, was totally unable to work, and had to be taken home by David Niven, an old friend who happened to be nearby at the time. Obviously she had to be replaced in the film. At this juncture Olivier was called, and arrived in Hollywood to a scene of total confusion. Since her breakdown she had been living in the company of an old flame, equally mad in everyone's opinion, until Niven and Stewart Granger had forcibly ejected him from the house. Now she was relatively calm, though she confided to Olivier on his arrival 'I'm in love, with . . . Peter Finch.' The only thing to do was to get her home as quickly and quietly as possible.

With Peter Finch, Dana Andrews and friend, on their way back from Ceylon after location shooting on Elephant Walk

Easier said than done. She had developed a terror of flying; she also had a terror of needles, so it was a nightmare to sedate her, and even when it was done she had an amazing resistance to the drugs used. Also, she was a world celebrity, and so was Olivier. Up to now, though it was fairly well known in the profession that she had psychological or 'nervous' problems, little word of it had leaked out to the public: now there was no way of keeping it secret. Olivier did the best he could, the American authorities were incredibly helpful, and she managed to arrive in London shaky but on her own two feet, to be whisked off at once to a sanatorium for treatment. This consisted first of prolonged sleep, then of electro-shock treatments, which, Olivier was informed, would probably be required intermittently for the rest of her life. Realising there was nothing further he could do at this point, he went off to resume his interrupted rest in Italy.

It must have seemed to everyone that Vivien would never work again. But if so they reckoned without her iron will and extraordinary powers of recuperation. She returned to Notley by mid-April, and continued to rest as much as possible. But 1953 was Coronation Year, and Olivier as a manager had been very eager to put on something special to mark the occasion as the two Cleopatras had Festival Year. While Vivien was convalescing he ran into Terence Rattigan, and on the off-chance asked if he might be working on something suitable. Rattigan replied that he was, and produced *The Sleeping Prince*, a comedy about the romantic-sideline affair of a mature Ruritanian prince with a London showgirl. Though Olivier was not so sure that it was one of Rattigan's better works, it was close to an ideal vehicle. Vivien thought likewise and by the autumn, incredibly, they were ready to open, first on tour and then in November (a little belatedly for the Coronation, to be sure) in London. On the whole the notices went this time to her rather than to him: she had the speed and lightness to skate over the surfaces as the play required; he was felt to take it too seriously and in consequence slow things down rather. But at least the Oliviers were back, and if the play was no runaway success, it managed to run respectably enough for five fairly restful months.

It was about this time that Olivier realised the quality of his own feelings had changed: the unthinkable had happened – he was no longer in love with Vivien. Possibly it was four years of her changed attitude to him, ranging from the sisterly to the furiously hostile. It might be that her nature had changed, through the passage of years, the acceleration of her illness, or even, as he tended to believe, the electro-shock treatments. But now the emotional stand-off was mutual. They continued to live and work together, but essentially they inhabited two separate worlds. They still entertained grandly at Notley, though their friends were nowadays mostly in separate groups. Vivien's affair with Peter Finch continued, in what seems to have been a rather desultory fashion, and when her attacks came on, as they did

Left: *with Laurence Olivier in* The Sleeping Prince *on stage*. Below: *Olivier and Vivien greet the star of the film version, Marilyn Monroe*

with some regularity, she was able to sit them out at Notley, often in the company of her mother. Few of their friends suspected the true seriousness of her condition, though quite often their adoration was likely to be mixed with irritation: plenty of both, for example, are to be found in Noël Coward's diaries of the 1950s. For those who had not known her before, the picture was likely to be rather different. Early in 1955, with the blessing of her doctors who believed that absorption in work was the best possible treatment for her, she undertook to appear in another Rattigan project, the film of his great stage success *The Deep Blue Sea*. We know that her co-star, Kenneth More, who had not come into close contact with her before, disliked her heartily and had no opinion of her charm, her intelligence or even her professionalism.

Casting her in the role was rather a curious idea anyway, since Hester is supposed to be a drab, defeated woman caught between two suicide attempts in a relationship very like Anna Karenina's with Vronsky after she has left her husband – a social outcast bound exclusively to a man who loves her well enough according to his lights, but cannot live on her lofty plane of all-for-love and still wants to go out to the pub and have a few drinks with the boys from time to time. It might have worked if Vivien had seen it all as a challenge, but the film treatment opened out the claustrophobic one-set play with wide-screen visits to ski-slopes in Switzerland and the Farnborough Air Show, and Vivien, according to More, cared about nothing except looking beautiful

Above: *with husband (Emlyn Williams) and lover (Kenneth More) in* The Deep Blue Sea. *20th Century Fox/London Films.* Above right: *clothes shopping in Paris, 1954*

and glamorous, and being constantly complimented on her looks and her clothes. Something of their (apparently mutual) dislike shows on screen, so that one has difficulty in accepting the consuming nature of this great love, and Vivien remains throughout amazingly unruffled by all that happens to her. But at least she got through the shooting without mishap, and that was about all anyone could have hoped for at this point in her career.

And it did offer some sort of guarantee for the next enterprise: a season at Stratford-upon-Avon in which she and Olivier would play in *Twelfth Night*, *Macbeth* and – an eccentric choice indeed – the rarely performed piece of early Shakespeare *grand guignol Titus Andronicus*. The reactions of the critics to all of these were decidedly curious. In his autobiography Olivier gallantly and not altogether inaccurately asserts that, for no rhyme or reason, critics will decide at any given time to idolise one performer and treat another as their whipping-boy; the only thing to do about it is to be philosophical and wait till the roles are reversed, as sooner or later they inevitably will be. At this time, and for this reason (or lack of reason), Olivier was riding high with the critics and Vivien could do little right. Even her enchanting Viola in *Twelfth Night* was grudgingly received, while attention was concentrated on Olivier's controversial new reading of Malvolio as a rather likeable fellow, even though a few thought it toppled the careful structure of the play. With *Macbeth* the critics were in full cry, particularly Kenneth Tynan: Olivier's Macbeth was definitive, but Vivien's Lady Macbeth was hopelessly insubstantial, quite lacking the force and the fury the role needed.

Some years later, when he was working on the script of Polanski's film *Macbeth*, Tynan told me he thought that was one of the worst errors of judgment he had ever made. In retrospect the combination of Olivier and Vivien, with its emphasis on the way Macbeth is held in sexual thrall by his lady and so will do anything to please her, made more sense of the play than any other reading he had seen, unconventional though it was in terms of the usual battle-axe interpretation of Lady M. But at the time the reviews were quite devastating, and Tynan's more so than anyone else's. Again, the profession does not seem to have shared these views, and it is interesting to note how many of those who bothered to answer Alan Dent's questionnaire about Vivien shortly after her death picked the Lady Macbeth as one of her supreme achievements.

Still, the Oliviers and the season soldiered on with *Titus Andronicus*, an extraordinary bloodbath which involves endless stabbings, rapes, mutilations (Titus loses a hand, his daughter Lavinia has both her hands and her tongue removed by her ravishers) and a final banquet where the evil empress unknowingly eats her two sons baked in a pie. Vivien was Lavinia, and consequently, since all the misfortunes befall her in the second act, had to play most of the evening in dumb show. Not, as Alan Dent remarked, any spirited actress's idea of fun. But the whole

Overleaf: (left) *Lavinia in* Titus Andronicus, *before mutilation;* (right): *Lady Macbeth with sex appeal*

thing was directed by Peter Brook with much spirit and appealed vastly to European audiences, particularly Parisian, on an extended European tour two years later. What effect this parade of horrors had on Vivien's precarious mental state we can only guess, but perhaps very little, since she seems never to have taken it very seriously in the first place. All the sticky moments of the season, at least, were off-stage, and it was not until it was all over that Vivien showed serious signs of collapse, tried to run off with Peter Finch and then pulled the train's communication cord and went back home again to one of her worst-ever manic attacks.

It was in the midst of this Stratford season, on 19 August to be precise, that the Oliviers' old friend Noël Coward, after a 'gloomy little visit', confided this view of their situation to his diary: *

Personally I think that if Larry had turned sharply on Vivien years ago and given her a clip in the chops, he would have been spared a mint of trouble. The seat of all this misery is our old friend, feminine ego. She is, and has been, thoroughly spoiled. She also has a sharp tongue and a bad temper. This, coupled with incipient TB and an inner certainty that she can never be as good an artist as Larry, however much she tries, had bubbled up in her and driven her on to the borderline. Fond as I am of her and sorry as I feel for her, I would like to give her a good belting, although now I fear it might push her over the edge and be far, far too late.

All the same, Coward, despite his moments of impatience with Vivien and distress over this image of the Oliviers 'trapped by public acclaim, scrabbling about in the cold ashes of a physical passion that burnt itself out years ago', offered Vivien the leading role in his new play, *South Sea Bubble*, to go into production early in 1956. Actually it was not all that new. It was written as *Home and Colonial* in 1949, revised and retitled *Island Fling* for a try-out in Westport, Connecticut in 1951 (with Claudette Colbert in the role eventually played by Vivien) then withdrawn for further revision before reaching its final form, and even at that it was not exactly vintage Coward. But it gave Vivien a nice showy role as the wife of a colonial governor who is beautiful, witty, turns all heads and has a spectacular drunk scene (with dance) with one of the natives under her husband's rule before all is comfortably sorted out in a rather tame conclusion. It must also have seemed providential coming up at this time, since Olivier had just been made an embarrassing offer he could hardly refuse. Marilyn Monroe's production company had bought the film rights to *The Sleeping Prince* and approached Olivier to re-create his original role on screen opposite Marilyn in the Vivien Leigh role. It would have been understandable if someone far more balanced than Vivien at this time had not taken too kindly to the idea. But with her busy too the difficult patch could be respectably glided over.

South Sea Bubble opened in Manchester on 19 March and arrived in London on 25 April. The critics were unenthusiastic

*The Noël Coward Diaries ed Graham Payn and Sheridan Morley, Weidenfeld & Nicolson, 1982.

about Coward's part in the evening (he was at that time the play-wright whipping-boy), but mostly enjoyed Vivien, and the show settled down to a run of 276 performances, very decidedly a personal success for her. Meanwhile, the setting-up of Olivier's film, rapidly retitled *The Prince and the Showgirl*, was surrounded with the same publicity as everything the ineffable MM did. When Marilyn came to England with her husband Arthur Miller to start shooting she and Vivien made a conventional show of being the best of friends, and though it was conventionally assumed that Vivien must be jealous she knew very well that in fact Olivier found Marilyn tiresome and difficult to deal with, since she was almost as neurotic as Vivien and by no means so capable of controlling it in professional situations.

In any case, even in terms of publicity Vivien was able to steal a march on Marilyn – just as filming was about to start she announced that she was four months pregnant. The pregnancy is one of the most mysterious episodes in Vivien's life. She was forty-two, showed no signs of pregnancy, and after another month it was announced that she had had a miscarriage and must rest completely (she had already left *South Sea Bubble*). Was she actually pregnant? It has been widely suggested that she was not, and this was just a strategic announcement. And yet all the evidence from Olivier, who should know, is that the pregnancy was perfectly genuine, deliberately entered into to help salvage both the marriage and her mental state (which sounds weird when one considers she had shown scant signs of maternal instinct with Suzanne), and that her doctors were all for their trying again as soon as she had had time to recover from the miscarriage. Apparently she was the one who lost interest or hope, and another door closed.

The year 1956 saw a series of rapid changes in the British theatre and both the Oliviers had to adapt to the new situation if they could. Fortunately it was not long before they each had a spectacular new success, though in Olivier's case a success which brought with it a more radical change in his personal life than he would ever have thought possible. The first, though not the only, cause for the theatrical changes was a twenty-six-year-old actor named John Osborne, who had a play called *Look Back in Anger* staged at the Royal Court in May 1956. Technically it contained few innovations, but the tone was new, and its success opened the theatre to a lot of new talents, some of them 'angry young men', as the phrase went, many of them young but not definably angry about anything. And with them came a whole new generation of actors who could convincingly play working-class characters and who turned their backs on the la-di-da upper-class diction which had long been *de rigueur* for London actors.

Of course Shakespeare and Shaw and Chekhov and Ibsen were still there, and the established greats, the knights and dames of the theatre, did not have to have anything to do with these new upstarts if they did not want to. But Olivier, after some soul-searching and initially unfavourable reactions, determined that he did want to. By a curious coincidence John Osborne was then working on a play about a broken-down music-hall comic which could be a perfect, though unexpected, vehicle for him: *The Entertainer*. No role in it, though, for Vivien, who was still far too young and attractive to play his raddled, sloppy old wife – even fantasies about special rubber face masks did not take them much farther. In any case, who said they must appear together? Critics indeed had been saying for years that they should not. So Olivier decided to go ahead with his adventure into the New Drama alone. He was the first of the great British classical actors to do so, and scored one of the major triumphs of his career in Osborne's play, first at the Royal Court for a short run, then later in the West End, in New York, and on film. And in the first Royal Court run there was, playing the role of his daughter, a young and little-known actress called Joan Plowright, whom Olivier had seen and found fascinating in the Royal Court's recent revival of *The Country Wife*. Though he did not realise it then, before the year was out they would be in love.

Meanwhile his relations with Vivien were reaching a point of no return. The long-delayed European tour of *Titus Andronicus*, taking in Paris, Vienna, Belgrade, Zagreb and Warsaw during the months of May and June, was a nightmare behind the scenes, with Vivien subject to violent ups and downs which seemed to be exacerbated by long hours in hot and crowded trains. On their return to London there was something further to get her worked up: the St James's Theatre was condemned, quite rightly in Olivier's opinion, as a fire trap which only the expenditure of an uneconomical quarter of a million could bring up to basic safety requirements. It was highly unlikely that any mad bene-factor would appear to do this, and so it was doomed to demolition. But Vivien made it a major cause, organising marches and protests and even interrupting a debate in the House of Lords before she was forcibly ejected. Quite possibly the strain of playing *Titus Andronicus* for a short London season did not help her state of mind either, and she retired afterwards to Notley in a trough of deep depression.

Shortly before this Olivier had decided, after coming seriously to blows with her over his recent attachment to another woman, that there was no way he could continue to deal with her or do her any good, and had quietly moved out. Rumours of divorce were rife, but no separation was made public, and when a headline-hunting MP demanded that a 'flood of indignation' should sweep the country because Vivien had gone on holiday with her daughter Suzanne and ex-husband Leigh while Olivier was holidaying in Scotland with his son Tarquin, they both firmly denied any split. But the writing was on the wall, and the collapse of two more joint ventures, a film of *Macbeth* and a Hollywood version of Rattigan's *Separate Tables* starring them both, put paid to any serious hopes of reconciliation. Then,

Marching to save their theatre

during the tour preceding the West End opening of *The Entertainer*, Olivier was forced to acknowledge that he was in love with Joan Plowright and she with him. She had to leave the play's cast to appear in two Ionecso plays in New York, but once the London run was ended he would be following her, taking *The Entertainer* to New York also.

Vivien seemed, to others and no doubt herself, to be abandoned and alone. But at this point her career too looked up: she was offered a meaty role in *Duel of Angels*, Christopher Fry's translation of Giraudoux's last, not quite completed play *Pour Lucrèce*. The duel in question is between two beautiful women, the wicked, vibrant Paola and the pallid, virtuous Lucile, whom Paola eventually drives to suicide. It is a curious piece: André Maurois said that act one was pure Giraudoux, act two *The Count of Monte Cristo* and act three all-out Victor Hugo melodrama. In French, with Edwige Feuillère and Madeleine Renaud playing the roles played by Vivien and Claire Bloom respectively in the English production, it worked perfectly. In English, Giraudoux generally ran into difficulties, since his plays, to English ears, were all style and precious little content, and they tended to get bogged down in the measured pace English actors characteristically adopt when required to project seriousness. But not, triumphantly not, when Vivien Leigh was in charge. Her peculiarly gallic skill in putting over lines at breakneck speed without losing clarity, weight or subtlety of pacing came completely into its own. Her Paola was all fire and ice, perverse passions and steely control. And she looked gorgeous, dressed in stark mid-nineteenth-century elegance by Dior. The production was an enormous personal success for her, restoring her to critical favour when she most needed it, and later she was to play the same role to similar acclaim in New York (1960) and on tour through Australia, New Zealand and Latin America (1961–62).

For the time being, however, her life went on much as usual with occasional outbreaks of mania or fits of depression, but now she knew how to fit them into the continuity of her professional life – on several occasions she would turn up for a performance of *Duel of Angels* still with the burn-marks on her forehead from an electro-shock treatment earlier in the day. During a short holiday from *Duel of Angels* she met Olivier in France (he had come back briefly from America), but his presence seemed to set her off in a manic spiral again and it became evident that they were better apart. In any case, rumours of his liaison with Joan Plowright were filtering back, though nothing definite had been stated in public. During the run of *Duel of Angels* Vivien turned forty-five and shortly after became a grandmother – Suzanne, who had married an insurance broker called Farrington the previous December, gave birth to a son.

When *Duel of Angels* closed she returned to Notley, and again became the glittering hostess of times past. Dirk Bogarde recalls an incident at one of the house parties which gives one a very

After her estrangement from Laurence Olivier, Vivien goes to the theatre with Robert Helpmann

A glamorous grandmother, with grandson Neville and (left) *daughter Suzanne*

Duel of Angels (right *and* opposite) *with Peter Wyngarde, dresses by Dior. Angus McBean*

clear picture of both Vivien's charm and her formidability: 'I suddenly remember another time at Notley when my beloved chum Kay Kendall was staying there, and was one evening behaving rather tiresomely, picking and niggling and being naughty generally. And Viv suddenly said, with the sweetest, blinding smile, and that soft, pussycat voice "Katie darling, if you are trying to pick a quarrel with me, don't. I shall win!"' No one who knew her could doubt for a moment the truth of that statement. As with Scarlett O'Hara, a generous, loyal, affectionate nature did not prevent her from being at times a beautiful bitch.

Early in 1959 her faithful stand-by Noël Coward offered Vivien another role, this time in something he had concocted specially with her in mind. *Look After Lulu* was a translation-adaptation of

Television debut in a new production of The Skin of Our Teeth, *1959*

No French farce would be complete without the heroine in her underwear: Look After Lulu

Feydeau's clockwork French farce *Occupe-toi d'Amélie*, and was a curious compromise at best, since in the process of adaptation Coward had decorated the intricate mechanics of the original with characteristic one-liners of his own which overweighted and distracted attention from the delicately balanced structure created by Feydeau. They were two different and, on this evidence, inimical forms of farcical humour, each cutting awkwardly across the other. But the role of Lulu d'Arville, the cocotte whose schemings and confusions propel the plot along at breakneck speed, fitted Vivien like a glove, and she was irresistible even if the play was not. It opened at the Royal Court – oddly considering that this was the scene of the New Drama's major triumphs, including *The Entertainer* – in July 1959, transferred to the West

End for a respectable if not spectacular run in September (largely on the strength of Vivien's drawing-power as a star) and to New York in April 1960. Merial Forbes (Lady Richardson), who was also in the cast, recalls that during much of the run of this featherweight trifle Vivien was in a bad way off-stage, tearful and depressed, and yet 'when we met on the stage at the opening of the play, she faced me like a little lioness, glittering eyes, a steely composure, her professional discipline turned on like a light'.

To add to her troubles, her father died just before Christmas, 1959, and her main contact with Olivier during the year was a business conference to discuss the possibility of selling Notley, which she had grown to love almost more than he did. The New York season of *Look After Lulu* brought her personal praise, but was not otherwise a success. After it, fortunately, someone had the happy idea of putting on *Duel of Angels* in New York, in a new production by Robert Helpmann (originally it had been directed by Jean-Louis Barrault) and with a new supporting cast, including, as Paola's husband, the same Jack Merivale who had, back in 1940, been the sufferer from one of the first definable bouts of Vivien's manic hysteria. It was to be a significant reunion. But before its significance could be fully appreciated, something else had to happen, and during the New York run of *Duel of Angels* it did: on 19 May 1960 she received a letter from Olivier telling her all about Joan Plowright and requesting a divorce. Before the day was out she had made her own statement to the press: 'Lady Olivier wishes to say that Sir Laurence has asked for a divorce in order to marry Miss Joan Plowright. She will naturally do whatever he wishes.' Though there were still several months of legal formalities to be sorted out, the romance of the century was now officially over.

After the Ball

The significance of Jack Merivale is, quite simply and sentimentally, that he brought Vivien love and understanding at the time when she was most desperately in need of it. Even as a grandmother, she was a beautiful and desirable woman, though she had increasing difficulty in believing it and needed constant reassurance. The fear of growing old and losing her charms was added to all the other psychological problems besetting her, and she was frequently heard to make remarks like her comment to Leigh on Eva Peron: 'A lucky thing she was. She died at thirty-two. I'm already forty-five.' Of course, she wanted to be contradicted, but fewer were dutifully ready to argue the point as her increasing tiresomeness alienated more and more old friends, like Noël Coward, who were basically sympathetic but did not know the extent of her mental health troubles or, if they did, found that sadly *tout comprendre* was not necessarily *tout pardonner*. With her own precipitate announcement that she was willing to give Olivier a divorce – it took him by surprise as the first answer he got to his letter was through reporters battering on his door – she severed the last link and cut herself adrift from all hope of a reconciliation. From now on, she was on her own.

Except for Jack. He and she had scarcely met for twenty years, so the instant spark at their first meeting in New York to start rehearsing the new production of *Duel of Angels* took them both by surprise. Jack did not know any more than anyone else about the state of the Oliviers' marriage, or for that matter her health problems, physical and psychological. But gradually a number of uncomfortable truths became evident. Even after their affair had begun during rehearsals, Vivien might say that she loved him, but seemed to be still obsessed with Olivier. And her moods became more and more uncontrollable – a mad see-saw of depression and elation, which curiously, increased in intensity after the triumphant opening. She was drinking, refusing to sleep and flying into inexplicable rages or sunk in gloom. On stage she always managed to stay in control, but off she was desperately unpredictable. She admitted to Jack what was the matter with her, adding 'Why can't I have a decent, clean illness?' And soon Irene Selznick was sent, as an emissary from Olivier, to tell him anything he did not already know and arrange for Vivien to have electro-shock treatment, which did not for some reason have as beneficial an effect as in England, leaving her with blinding headaches.

When Olivier's request for divorce came, Jack was on hand, and in the following weeks Vivien became more dependent on him than ever, and more loving. The play was closed by an Equity strike and the producer decided to tour it to Los Angeles, San Francisco, Chicago and Washington instead of reopening in New York, which enabled Vivien to go back to England for treatment and gave Jack some time to think. Her return and the start of the tour took care of any doubts he may have had: for all her problems, he loved her; she seemed to love him; and in June

Mrs Stone contemplates autumn.
Warner Bros

The Roman Spring of Mrs Stone. Above: *serenaded with Warren Beatty.* Left: *ex-actress Karen Stone (Vivien Leigh) being prepared for one of her stage appearances. Warner Bros*

he wrote to Olivier to tell him so and, in effect, to take over responsibility for her. The whole tour went off without a hitch or a recurrence of her attacks, and at its conclusion they took ship for Europe, first stop Paris, where Vivien was to have fittings at Balmain for the wardrobe of her next film, *The Roman Spring of Mrs Stone*, adapted from the novel by Tennessee Williams and to be made supposedly in Rome, though in the event shooting was shifted to Elstree.

Before work began on the film two divorce petitions were heard and granted the same day by the same court: Roger Gage's against his actress-wife Joan Plowright, with Laurence Olivier cited as co-respondent, and Vivien's against Olivier with Joan Plowright as co-respondent. It was all neat and easy and soon over. The shooting of the film, in which Vivien played a sister to Blanche Dubois, a rich, recently widowed ex-actress falling apart in Rome as her long repressed libido drives her along an increasingly self-destructive course, also went in the main without a hitch. Vivien did not always see eye to eye with her young co-star Warren Beatty, though she was extremely impressed by his talent as well as his sex appeal, and in compensation the inexperienced director Jose Quintero was easy to manipulate, so she got her own way a lot. She managed, for instance, to get leave from the shooting to go to Atlanta for a gala preview of *Gone With the Wind* newly topped and tailed for the wide screen (she and Olivia de Havilland were by now the only important survivors), and on the way had a meeting, very stiff and formal, with Olivier and Joan Plowright, who were then both starring on the Broadway stage. Shortly after her return it was announced that they had got married in New York, and Vivien took it like a trouper. Despite what might have been a nasty riding accident, she finished the film only a little behind schedule, and proved to have given one of her best performances, even if the film itself was not great.

Only afterwards did the reaction come, with some violent manic outbursts, but by now Jack had come to recognise the signs of their onset, and got her treated at an early stage. Again, work was the well-tried answer, and at the end of June 1961 they set off together on a long-planned Old Vic tour of the Antipodes, to which at the last minute Latin America was added, keeping them away in all for nearly a year. The repertory was mostly comfortably familiar to her – *Twelfth Night*, in which she again played Viola, and *Duel of Angels*, with only *The Lady of the Camellias* as a new role for her to master. It was, as it happened, one of her favourites among all her theatre roles, and to judge from the photographs (she never got to play it in Europe) she was looking incredibly beautiful and for once not self-conscious about stepping into Garbo's shoes – for unforgettable though Garbo might have been in *Camille*, could she have sustained the same role on stage, as part of a complex repertory during a gruelling international tour? The comparisons this time were all in Vivien's favour, and she knew it.

Rehearsing with Jack Merivale for the Old Vic Australian tour of Twelfth Night

Otherwise the history of the tour followed a pattern which by now was becoming painfully familiar: strict professional discipline and total professional success, but behind the scenes a terrifying switchback of mania and depression, impossible behaviour followed by contrition but no guarantee that it would not happen again. When a bout of mania was coming upon her, Vivien's first action, entirely unconscious, was to start systematically taking off all her jewellery – rings, bracelets, necklaces, ear-rings, everything – and laying it down neatly on a table. Then she would start compulsively cleaning something, anything. Once the rest of the cast grasped this pattern of behaviour, they started to do likewise, taking off jewellery and cleaning, so that even if she might feel crazy, she would not feel alone. Somehow they all got through it and returned to England in June 1962, still in one piece. Or, strictly speaking, in two. Though the attachment between Vivien and Jack was by now generally recognised and they spent most of their time together, they religiously maintained separate establishments and Vivien, in oracular mood, once confided to Tarquin Olivier 'Leigh taught me how to live, your father how to love, and Jack how to be alone.' This was not quite so dramatic as it sounded, but it did witness to a new independence in Vivien's attitude: in any clash, she had nearly always given in to Olivier, but now Jack nearly always gave in to her. She bought, on her own, a new country home, Tickeridge Mill in Sussex, to replace Notley on a much more intimate scale, and loved it dearly, even though she kept up a flat in Eaton Square to the end of her days.

She was to spend the rest of 1962 mostly down at Tickeridge, with a constant procession of visitors to keep her amused. But she would soon be off again. In Australia she had been sent the script of a new musical version of Jacques Deval's old light-comedy standby about impoverished Russian emigré aristocrats in Paris, *Tovarich*, and after some initial doubts about her ability to sing had let herself be persuaded. The show was set for production in March 1963, in New York, and she set off before Christmas without Jack, as he was appearing in a film in Britain at the time. Almost at once she was too busy to be ill, and even when she had a bad attack of depression in Philadelphia during the pre-Broadway tour she managed to keep things in proportion and to herself. When it opened in New York there were no reviews because of a prolonged newspaper strike, but the public lapped it up, and a spirited Charleston she had to dance could be relied on to get a standing ovation every night. Not only that, but when the time for the Tonys, Broadway's Oscars, came round, still before the strike was settled, she won one for the best performance by an actress in a musical. When the critics were finally heard again, all they could very well do was to endorse the public's verdict: she was delightful, her co-star Jean-Pierre Aumont was the epitome of gallic charm, and the show would just about do.

It might have gone on doing for a very long time. But during

Opposite: *duchess with a duster, Tovarich*

Above: *rehearsing with Byron Mitchell for her show-stopping Charleston in* Tovarich. Left: *with Jean-Pierre Aumont recording the cast album*

the miserable New York summer her condition deteriorated rapidly, and by the time Jack arrived to appear in a new production of *The Importance of Being Earnest* she was close to total disintegration. Her manic fits were more physically violent than ever, and in them she was quite capable of destroying every object within reach and severely lacerating anyone who tried to restrain her. Performances went on as usual but finally even that became too much for her. She collapsed in the middle of a performance, and had to be shipped back to England for treatment.

This time it really could have been the end. Ever the arch-professional, she was becoming notoriously unreliable, and producers, reasonably enough, hesitated to invest money in her. Moreover she did not need to work as she was very well off (though her friends did not think so), having earned a lot and invested wisely, so that she could easily afford her extravagant life-style and personal generosity. But the urge could not be stilled. Determined as ever, she rested at Tickeridge and planned. She wanted to do *Tovarich* in London; she wanted to make a television special of *The Lady of the Camellias*; she was full of ideas, though none of them seemed anywhere near fruition. Then, while she was on holiday with Jack in Tobago, an offer came from Stanley Kramer for her to play one of the leading roles in his all-star adaptation of Katherine Anne Porter's bestselling

A drunken dance in Ship of Fools. *Columbia*

novel *Ship of Fools*. It was a meaty role, if for her perhaps a trifle on the masochistic side, as Mrs Treadwell, another of those aging, once-beautiful women cast adrift by life and trying to remain dignified and human whatever humiliations experience may offer them. The film was to be shot entirely in a Hollywood studio in June 1964, and she readily accepted.

It was to be her last film, her last visit to Hollywood, and her last notable success. She was surrounded by old friends, particularly George Cukor and Katharine Hepburn, who found a house for her up in the Hollywood Hills. She tended to mania on and off throughout the shooting, but shock treatments kept it under reasonable control. She had her clashes with other members of the cast, particularly the most important other female star, Simone Signoret. Basically she disapproved of Signoret for letting her figure go and lacking personal discipline, and when there were embarrassing disagreements over the apportioning of the expenses for a cast party they jointly threw (Vivien's ideas were far too extravagant for Signoret's bourgeois principles of economical management) there was a permanent stand-off between them. All the same, she got through the film with a minimum of disruption, and though she was subsequently outraged to find that one of her key scenes had been left on the cutting-room floor, by general consent she provided the only bright spot in a very stodgy and pretentious confection. By then she must have been heartily sick of being adjudged the sole saviour of inferior material.

The American writer Peter Feibleman, who knew her slightly, tells an interesting story about this period in Hollywood which illustrates that there was often method, and a strange kind of perceptiveness, in her madness. He visited her shortly after she had arrived in her rented house, to find her in a curious mood of dislocation: her opening line was 'I suppose I'm here. Are you?' She was restless, and admitted to an irrational feeling that something was wrong, something horrible was going on somewhere. Then suddenly she vanished, and Feibleman discovered her deep in the camellia bushes which bordered the terrace, savagely tearing off all the blooms. Manic destructiveness? No, she had just realised precisely what was wrong – they were all plastic, pinned on to real bushes. Once nature had been deloused, she was much happier and reassured. '*I know* I'm here now. I feel lots better. It takes a while to be able to see in a place like this.'

Her problem in life was often precisely that she saw too clearly for her own good. The rest of her story can be quickly told. Early in 1965 she was going through a relatively calm patch, and was approached by an American producer with the idea of doing on stage a play called *The Contessa*, adapted by Paul Osborn from a novel, *The Film of Memory*, by Maurice Druon. It was about a dotty old contessa who was once the most loved woman in Europe: a different version had been a great success for Elvire Popescu on the Paris stage, and it was felt to have good film prospects (though when eventually it was filmed, as *A Matter of*

The role London never saw: The Contessa *on tour*

Time, with Ingrid Bergman in Vivien's part, the results were disastrous). It suited Vivien's mood to go from her familiar beauty to the other extreme of grotesqueness, and she accepted, but the production never really came together, and closed after a try-out tour without ever coming to London. Next she was asked to take over opposite Gielgud as the betrayed Jewish wife in the American production of Chekhov's *Ivanov*, since the actress who had played it originally in Britain was not available. She did so, and again got excellent notices, though the run was limited and her part, though quite showy, was small, as she dies of tuberculosis during the interval.

That was in May and June 1966. She returned home to Tickeridge decidedly unwell, physically rather than mentally this time, and did actually rest and look after herself throughout the winter. In the spring she was offered a leading role in Edward Albee's new play *A Delicate Balance*, which was to go into rehearsal during the summer and start on tour in the early autumn before opening in London. She professed mystification as to what her role, let alone the play, was about, but accepted nevertheless and began to work on the text with her co-star Michael Redgrave. In June she came up to the Eaton Square flat, and suddenly started to lose weight dramatically and spit blood. It transpired that her tuberculosis had flared up again, and now affected both lungs. She refused to go into hospital; her doctor prescribed complete rest for three months, and she agreed. But it was too late. On 7 July Jack left her for a few moments and came back into her room to find that she had got up, struggled towards the bathroom, and died before she could get there. She was fifty-three, and still Scarlett O'Hara, only now she had at last run out of tomorrows.

Lass Unparallel'd

In a way, of course, Alexander Korda was right about Vivien Leigh, way back in 1935. He knew where he was with his three current female stars; each of them had a clear and simple type. Merle Oberon was the exotic, Wendy Barrie was the pure English rose, and Diana Napier was the bitch. He rejected Vivien because she did not fall into any neat category. He thought at the time that this was because she had no real personality; later he realised that it was because she had too much, or too many. Was she exotic, a virgin-next-door, or a bitch? A bit of all of them, and none of them completely. That was a large part of her fascination. She could certainly be a bitch in her private life, as many discovered if they happened to catch her in a bad mood or got the rough side of her tongue – though more often she could quell people better by a lethal, feline smoothness. She might even have been the girl-next-door, though most of us should be so lucky as to find someone of such extraordinary and spectacular looks blooming unseen just the other side of the garden fence. And exotic without doubt she was. Though the overriding impression she created was intensely English, there were many disturbing undertones in the contrast of the dark hair and the pale creamy complexion, the green eyes set at an angle, and the heart-shaped face with the high cheekbones and the full lips which curled intriguingly upwards at the corners. Everything suggested that this pussycat, quietly purring, could be a wildcat when roused – and so, evidently, she was.

In addition to all this she was a wit, a highly intelligent person, and a lady. And a professional. Except on the very rarest of occasions – only two, to my knowledge – even her severest bouts of mania or depression were not allowed in any way to affect her work. She might be an incoherent wreck off-stage, but as soon as she stepped on she was herself, immaculate and unflappable for the duration of the performance, even if then she went right back to where she was before. That is professionalism, on an almost superhuman scale, but it also had a lot to do with what made her, to use correctly that much-abused term, a lady. Her ladylikeness had most to do with an inner sense of proportion and propriety: she could, if she wished, swear like a trooper, and did so, but she always picked her moment or timed everything as meticulously as she would arrange a vase of flowers or place an Impressionist just so on a wall.

It is impossible to tell where this extraordinary combination of qualities came from. One can always invoke the suspicious tangle of ancestry, the French and the Irish, the unmentioned Dutch and the late-discovered Spanish, but one might as well blame it all on her mother's superstitious glances towards Kanchenjunga before her birth. Ultimately she was what she was, and she made herself that way, if only, perhaps, at cost to her sanity. As an actress, too, she created herself, working tirelessly on technical questions like how to find the right voice for Shakespeare's Cleopatra as well as Shaw's. On screen her unique personality was a great help. When she was well cast, as in *Gone With the Wind*, *A Streetcar Named Desire* and *Ship of Fools* especially, she hardly had to play the role at all, just be it. In this she was a true movie star, and a great one. But she could also act in the more traditional sense, transforming herself on stage by finding elements of any character's truth in her own being, but using them to fashion a persona that was clearly not her own face. Though I was too young to see her in *The Skin of Our Teeth*, I can testify that the image of her in *Macbeth*, *South Sea Bubble*, *Duel of Angels* and *Look After Lulu* remains indelibly with me now, as clear and unforgettable as anything I ever saw in close-up on the silver screen. Very likely she could not do everything that, say, Peggy Ashcroft or Edith Evans could do, but then they could not do everything she could do, and in her combination of seriousness and speed, lightness and precision, she was unique among English actresses of her day, or any other as far as I know.

Was she a really nice person, a truly warm and wonderful human being? Quite possibly not: everything was too mercilessly bathed in the cold clear light of her intelligence for that. Athene Seyler, most perceptive of observers, had from the outset an impression of her made up of 'directness, and lack of affectation, and a candid simplicity of personality,' and adds 'I liked her reliability, her straightforwardness, and her good manners which sprang from a lucid impersonal interest in people'. Note that 'impersonal' – there was always something oddly detached about her, which in many ways contributed to the image she gave of being 'invisibly spotlit' (Garson Kanin's phrase), but also helped to keep people, and life, at arm's length. This was not entirely an alienating quality, because if she sometimes seemed to be the other side of a sheet of plate-glass, it also seemed that she was as eager, indeed sometimes desperate, to break through it as was the rest of the world to get through to her and penetrate her mystery.

Even nearly twenty years after her death, it is this teasing, ambiguous quality which still makes it impossible to dismiss her from mind. With her it is truly, once seen, never forgotten, and as her films, even the once sacrosanct *Gone With the Wind*, turn up on television and video cassette, new generations in seemingly endless succession have the chance to see and remember. Katharine Hepburn once said that all truly great stars have and need the power to irritate. That Vivien had, and has, in full measure. Millions have loved her on screen; millions have also longed to shake a little sense into her. But one has to remember that it is the irritation to an oyster that produces the pearl, and the irritation a Vivien Leigh offers to the public is rapidly overlaid by the sheen of something rich and rare. There never was anyone remotely like her, and it seems safe to suppose that we shall not see her like again. Worship we may, but if any ghostly sound echoes from her, it is surely the tinkle of ironic laughter, putting our foolishness and solemnity in their place. With her, after all, the situation was always hopeless, and never serious.

Filmography

1934 **Things Are Looking Up** Dir: Albert De Courville. With Cicely Courtneidge, Dick Henderson, Dick Henderson Jr, Suzanne Lenglen.

1935 **The Village Squire** Dir: Reginald Denham. With Leslie Perrins, David Horne.
Gentleman's Agreement Dir: George Pearson. With Frederick Peisley, Antony Holles, David Horne, Ronald Shiner.
Look Up and Laugh Dir: Basil Dean. With Gracie Fields, Douglas Wakefield, Billy Nelson, Harry Tate, Robb Wilton, Kenneth More, Alfred Drayton, Maud Gill.

1937 **Fire Over England** Dir: William K. Howard. With Laurence Olivier, Flora Robson, Leslie Banks, Raymond Massey, Tamara Desni, Robert Newton, Donald Calthrop.
Dark Journey Dir: Victor Saville. With Conrad Veidt, Ursula Jeans, Anthony Bushell, Austin Trevor, Robert Newton, Cecil Parker.
Storm in a Teacup Dir: Victor Saville, Ian Dalrymple. With Rex Harrison, Cecil Parker, Sara Allgood, Ursula Jeans.

1938 **A Yank at Oxford** Dir: Jack Conway. With Robert Taylor, Lionel Barrymore, Maureen O'Sullivan, Griffith Jones, Edmund Gwenn, Edward Rigby.
St Martin's Lane (US title: **Sidewalks of London**) Dir: Tim Whelan. With Charles Laughton, Rex Harrison, Larry Adler, Tyrone Guthrie, Maire O'Neill, Basil Gill, Clare Greet, Helen Haye.

1939 **Twenty-One Days** (US title: **Twenty-One Days Together**) Made in 1937. Dir: Basil Dean (Alexander Korda uncredited). With Laurence Olivier, Leslie Banks, Francis L. Sullivan, Hay Petrie, Esme Percy, Robert Newton, David Horne.
Gone With the Wind Dir: Victor Fleming (George Cukor, Sam Wood and others uncredited). With Clark Gable, Olivia de Havilland, Leslie Howard, Thomas Mitchell, Victor Jory, Ward Bond, Hattie McDaniel, Butterfly McQueen, Barbara O'Neil, Evelyn Keyes, Ann Rutherford, Ona Munson, Laura Hope Crews.

1940 **Waterloo Bridge** Dir: Mervyn Le Roy. With Robert Taylor, Lucile Watson, Maria Ouspenskaya, C. Aubrey Smith, Virginia Field.

1941 **That Hamilton Woman!** (UK title: **Lady Hamilton**) Dir: Alexander Korda. With Laurence Olivier, Alan Mowbray, Sara Allgood, Gladys Cooper, Henry Wilcoxon, Heather Angel.

1945 **Caesar and Cleopatra** Dir: Gabriel Pascal. With Claude Rains, Flora Robson, Francis L. Sullivan, Cecil Parker, Stewart Granger, Raymond Lovell, Ernest Thesiger, Michael Rennie, Esme Percy, Stanley Holloway, Leo Genn.

1948 **Anna Karenina** Dir: Julien Duvivier. With Ralph Richardson, Kieron Moore, Sally Ann Howes, Niall MacGinnis, Martita Hunt, Marie Lohr, Michael Gough, Heather Thatcher, Helen Haye, Austin Trevor.

1951 **A Streetcar Named Desire** Dir: Elia Kazan. With Marlon Brando, Kim Hunter, Karl Malden, Ruby Bond, Nick Dennis.

1954 **Elephant Walk** Dir: William Dieterle. With Peter Finch, Dana Andrews, Abraham Sofaer. (VL was replaced halfway through shooting by Elizabeth Taylor, but is still visible in long-shots.)

1955 **The Deep Blue Sea** Dir: Anatole Litvak. With Kenneth More, Emlyn Williams, Eric Portman, Moira Lister, Arthur Hill, Miriam Karlin, Heather Thatcher, Dandy Nichols.

1961 **The Roman Spring of Mrs Stone** Dir: Jose Quintero. With Warren Beatty, Coral Browne, Lotte Lenya, Jeremy Spenser, Jill St John, Ernest Thesiger, Bessie Love, Cleo Laine.

1965 **Ship of Fools** Dir: Stanley Kramer. With Simone Signoret, Oskar Werner, Lee Marvin, Jose Ferrer, George Segal, Elizabeth Ashley, Heinz Ruhmann, Michael Dunn, Jose Greco, Charles Korvin.

Acknowledgements

The author and publishers would like to thank the following for permission to use copyright photographs in this book: frontispiece Angus McBean; p. 8 (left) G Coburn; p. 8 (right) Tunbridge; p. 9 (left) Leonard Waldorf; p. 9 (right), 85 Ted Reed; p. 13, 41, 47 (left), 83 (above) BBC Hulton Picture Library; p. 27 (above), 48, 61, 63 Culver Pictures Inc; p. 31, 36, 37 (bottom), 40, 74, 83 (bottom), 87, 96, 106 (top left), 108, 109, 115, 119, 121, colour section p. 6 (above left and above right) Popperfoto; p. 6, 99, 104, 105, 106 (above left), 114 (bottom), 126 Memory Shop; p. 32 Mrs Mary Brown; p. 42 Raymond Mander and Joe Mitchenson Theatre Collection; p. 51 V&A; p. 55, 58 (bottom) Laszlo Willinger; p. 123 Robert Coburn; colour section p. 3 Ronald Searle.

Special thanks also to William Kenly for his help.